MAGIC(AL) REALISM

Magic(al) Realism navigates the complexities of one of today's most popular genres within literature, art and film.

Maggie Ann Bowers:

- explores 'magic', 'magical' and 'marvellous' realism and the distinctions between the terms
- examines their origins in German post-expressionist painting and Latin American fiction
- analyses the relationship of magic(al) realism with other artistic movements, such as surrealism
- offers an historical overview of the geographical, cultural and political contexts within which the genre has developed
- considers the relationship of magic(al) realism to issues of post-colonialism, cross-culturalism and postmodernism
- illustrates her study with fresh readings of the work of eminent writers such as Salman Rushdie, Toni Morrison, Isabel Allende, Gabriel García Márquez and Angela Carter

This concise yet wide-ranging guide offers a clear way through confusing terms and debates to provide the ideal introduction to a fascinating field.

Maggie Ann Bowers is a Senior Lecturer at the University of Portsmouth where she teaches Literature in English, specializing in multi-ethnic and postcolonial writing of North America. She previously taught at the University of Antwerp and is the co-editor of *Convergences and Interferences: Newness in Intercultural Practices* (2002).

THE NEW CRITICAL IDIOM

SERIES EDITOR: JOHN DRAKAKIS, UNIVERSITY OF STIRLING

The New Critical Idiom is an invaluable series of introductory guides to today's critical terminology. Each book:

- provides a handy, explanatory guide to the use (and abuse) of the term
- offers an original and distinctive overview by a leading literary and cultural critic
- relates the term to the larger field of cultural representation.

With a strong emphasis on clarity, lively debate and the widest possible breadth of examples, *The New Critical Idiom* is an indispensable approach to key topics in literary studies.

Also available in this series:

To the memory of D. W. Jefferson

Contents

SERIES EDITOR'S PREFACE

The New Critical Idiom is a series of introductory books which seeks to extend the lexicon of literary terms, in order to address the radical changes which have taken place in the study of literature during the last decades of the twentieth century. The aim is to provide clear, well-illustrated accounts of the full range of terminology currently in use, and to evolve histories of its changing usage.

The current state of the discipline of literary studies is one where there is considerable debate concerning basic questions of terminology. This involves, among other things, the boundaries which distinguish the literary from the non-literary; the position of literature within the larger sphere of culture; the relationship between literatures of different cultures; and questions concerning the relation of literary to other cultural forms within the context of interdisciplinary structures.

It is clear that the field of literary criticism and theory is a dynamic and heterogeneous one. The present need is for individual volumes on terms which combine clarity of exposition with an adventurousness of perspective and a breadth of application. Each volume will contain as part of its apparatus some indication of the direction in which the definition of particular terms is likely to move, as well as expanding the disciplinary boundaries within which some of these terms have been traditionally contained. This will involve some re-situation of terms within the larger field of cultural representation, and will introduce examples from the area of film and the modern media in addition to examples from a variety of literary texts.

PREFACE

The writing of this book was motivated by the lack of an accessible English language guide to the confusing and often confused terms associated with magic(al) realism. The aim of this study is to guide the non-expert through the minefield of terms, to identify the origins of the terms and concepts in art, literature and film and to introduce readers to a range of innovative and engaging fiction. It differentiates the concept from other terms and genres, gives an overview of the geographical and cultural range of the fiction and explains the variants that have been identified by critics. Finally, it considers the future of the term in relation to postcolonial criticism and provides a useful bibliography and glossary.

ACKNOWLEDGEMENTS

In completing this book, I wish to thank the editors John Drakakis and Liz Thompson for their comments and encouragement. Thanks are also due for the expert advice of Monica Kendall, Katrien Vloeberghs, Rita de Maeseneer and Wendy Faris. As ever, I am grateful for the years of support and invaluable advice from Lyn Innes and Joris Duytschaever. Thanks also to my colleagues in the Postcolonial Research Group and the Department of Germanic Literature and Languages of the University of Antwerp for their friendship and support. The author gratefully acknowledges support from the University of Antwerp NOI research fund, Antwerpen 2000. I am forever indebted to my loving and patient family whose interest in the book kept me motivated even through piles of nappies and long sleepless nights.

INTRODUCTION

Since the 1980s, the terms 'magic realism', 'magical realism' and 'marvellous realism' have become both highly fashionable and highly derided. On the face of it, they are oxymorons describing the forced relationship of irreconcilable terms. It is in fact the inherent inclusion of contradictory elements that has made and sustained the usefulness and popularity of the concepts to which the terms refer. In recent years the term 'magical realism' has become the most popularly used one of the three terms, referring to a particular narrative mode. What the narrative mode offers is a way to discuss alternative approaches to reality to that of Western philosophy, expressed in many postcolonial and non-Western works of contemporary fiction by, most famously, writers such as Gabriel García Márquez and Salman Rushdie. It is this aspect that has made it most pertinent to late twentieth-century literature. However, the widespread use of the term among critics has brought with it its own problems. The popularity of such writing with the reading public has never been higher, but writers and critics are concerned that the terms are being reduced to vague clichés. Writers have been distancing themselves from the term whilst their publishers have increasingly used the terms to describe their works for marketing purposes. This book aims to provide a means to understand the origins of these terms, their differing usages, and provides a way for the reader to gain an understanding of the reasons behind the variety of strong reactions both for and against their use.

The one thing that the majority of critical works about the related terms 'magic realism', 'magical realism' and 'marvellous realism' agree upon is that these terms are notoriously difficult to define. This book offers a path through the critical minefield surrounding the terms as they are applicable to art, literature, film and television. It follows their history from the 1920s to the present day: from early twentieth-century German Art criticism to international contemporary literary criticism.

One of the main sources of confusion surrounding the terms is the lack of accuracy of their application. Each variation of the term has developed in specific and different contexts and yet they have become mistakenly interchangeable in critical usage. They have also gone through many variations of translation: the terms originated from the German *Magischer Realismus* which travelled and was translated into the Dutch *magisch-realisme*, the English 'magic realism' and eventually the Spanish *realismo mágico*. After its introduction, the term *lo real maravilloso* was translated from Spanish into both the terms 'marvellous realism' and 'marvellous reality'. Later again, the Spanish term *realismo mágico* was translated also to 'magical realism' and occasionally 'magico realism'. With each translation the connections between the terms and their origins become blurred and confused. However, it is possible to trace these origins and this is the subject of Chapter 1. The first of the terms, *Magischer Realismus* or magic realism, was coined in Germany in the 1920s in relation to the painting of the Weimar Republic that tried to capture the mystery of life behind the surface reality. The second of the terms, *lo real maravilloso* or marvellous realism, was introduced in Latin America during the 1940s as an expression of the mixture of realist and magical views of life in the context of the differing cultures of Latin America expressed through its art and literature. The third term, *realismo mágico* or magical realism was introduced in the 1950s in relation to Latin American fiction, but has since been adopted as the main term used to refer to all narrative fiction that includes magical happenings in a realist matter-of-fact narrative, whereby, 'the supernatural is not a simple or obvious matter, but it *is* an ordinary matter, and everyday occurrence – admitted, accepted, and integrated into the rationality and materiality of literary realism' (Zamora and Faris 1995: 3).

'Magic realism' or 'magical realism' are terms which many people have heard and yet very few readers have a clear idea of what they may include and imply. Much of the confusion concerning their meaning has occurred due to the conflation of criticism on 'magic realist' art and literature and that of 'magical realist' fiction. Although they have many features in common, the two terms refer to subtly different characteristics and influences. What follows aims to distinguish and disentangle these critical terms so that their meaning is clarified and their usage is meaningful. This book will distinguish between 'magic realism' as the concept of the 'mystery [that] does not descend to the represented world, but rather hides and palpitates behind it' (Roh 1995: 15) and 'magical realism' that is understood, in Salman Rushdie's words, as the 'commingling of the improbable and the mundane' (1982: 9).

For the purposes of discussing these works of art and literature where they have features in common the terms will be conflated in this book under the catch-all term of 'magic(al) realism'. The terms 'magic realism', 'magical realism' and 'marvellous realism' will also be used specifically to discuss their separate critical histories.

Critics still debate whether the terms refer to modes, genres or forms of writing, or simply cultural concepts. In fact, they are discussed most frequently in their widest senses as concepts of reality. Since the introduction in the 1950s of the terms 'marvellous realism' and 'magical realism' in relation to literature, critics have attempted to identify those aspects that define this type of fiction. Due to the variety of applications of these terms and their changing meanings, critics have found that it is difficult to consider them in terms of one unifying genre, but rather that they constitute particular narrative modes. The distinguishing feature of 'marvellous realism', for instance, is that its fiction brings together the seemingly opposed perspectives of a pragmatic, practical and tangible approach to reality and an acceptance of magic and superstition into the context of the same novel.

'Magical realism', which of all the terms has had the most critical consideration, relies most of all upon the matter-of-fact, realist tone of its narrative when presenting magical happenings. For this reason it is often considered to be related to, or even a version of literary realism.

Its distinguishing feature from literary realism is that it fuses the two opposing aspects of the oxymoron (the magical and the realist) together to form one new perspective. Because it breaks down the distinction between the usually opposing terms of the magical and the realist, magical realism is often considered to be a disruptive narrative mode. For this reason it is considered that 'magical realism is a mode suited to exploring . . . and transgressing . . . boundaries, whether the boundaries are onto-logical, political, geographical, or generic' (Zamora and Faris 1995: 5). The magical realist narrative mode is also considered by contemporary magical realist critics such as Amaryll Chanady to be a tolerant and accepting type of fiction. As Chanady explains, this narrative point of view relies upon an 'absence of obvious judgements about the veracity of the events and the authenticity of the world view expressed by characters in the text' (1985: 30). One of the unique features of magical realism is its reliance upon the reader to follow the example of the narrator in accepting both realistic and magical perspectives of reality on the same level. It relies upon the full acceptance of the veracity of the fiction during the reading experience, no matter how different this perspective may be to the reader's non-reading opinions and judgements.

Magical realism has become a popular narrative mode because it offers to the writer wishing to write against totalitarian regimes a means to attack the definitions and assumptions which support such systems (e.g. colonialism) by attacking the stability of the definitions upon which these systems rely. As the postcolonial critic Brenda Cooper notes, 'Magical realism at its best opposes fundamentalism and purity; it is at odds with racism, ethnicity and the quest for tap roots, origins and homogeneity' (1998: 22). This is the key to its recent popularity as a mode of fiction, particularly in Latin America and the postcolonial English-speaking world.

Rather than being a recent phenomenon that most people associate with the emergence of Latin American literature, the history of magic(al) realism stretches back to the early 1920s. Although the terms have gone through many and often radical changes of meaning, the resilience of the terms lies in their usefulness to describe a particular attitude to non-scientific and non-pragmatic beliefs in a world which is universally influenced by science and pragmatism. However, varying attitudes to the concept of magic produce a wide variety of magical realist and magic realist works. Magic and the magical are constructs created in particular cultural contexts. It follows that magic realism and magical realism have as many forms of magic and the magical in them as the number of cultural contexts in which these works are produced throughout the world. In magic realist and magical realist works of art 'magic' can be a synonym for mystery, an extraordinary happening, or the supernatural and can be influenced by European Christianity as much as by, for instance, Native American indigenous beliefs.

It is typical for books and essays on magic(al) realism to begin by stating that the concept and its history are too complex to be able to provide a definition. Most critics settle for a working definition outlined by a list of properties which, when included in a text, may be covered by the umbrella of the term. The purpose of this book is to provide an understanding of how these various working definitions are related, what the origins of the terms were and what does and does not constitute magic realism and magical realism. The aim of this analysis will be to produce a wider definition of the concept with which to understand the subtler differences of these variations of the concept it has come to encompass.

Chapter 1 is a guide to the origins and development of the terms from the Weimar Republic of Germany of the 1920s, to the 1940s and 1950s in Latin America and finally to the last three decades of the twentieth century in the English-speaking world. By following the developments of the terms chronologically, this chapter provides a way to understand their often confusingly different applications and nuances in relation to each other. Chapter 2 untangles the confusions surrounding the terms further by distinguishing other literary and artistic movements such as realism, surrealism, the fantastic and science fiction from magic(al) realism.

Chapters 3, 4 and 5 provide a guide to the variations of magical realist writing and the locations and circumstances in which they developed. These chapters will make particular reference to and analysis of important magical realist novels by writers such as Gabriel García Márquez, Salman Rushdie, Angela Carter, Günter Grass and Toni Morrison. Chapter 3 identifies and explains the development of magical realist writing in its various locations throughout the world including descriptions of their political, historical and artistic contexts. The chapter is divided into three sections dedicated to the locations of Latin America, the English-speaking world and mainland Europe. Chapters 4 and 5 continue the analysis of differing types of magical realist fiction and their relationship to various contemporary approaches of literary criticism. These chapters identify the importance of concepts such as transgression and the carnivalesque, postcolonialism, cross-culturalism, postmodernism and ontology to magical realism and the manner in which these concepts interrelate in magical realist writing. They continue the analysis from Chapter 3 of the works of writers such as Gabriel García Márquez, Salman Rushdie, Angela Carter, Isabel Allende and Toni Morrison. Chapter 6 outlines the occurrence of magic realism and magical realism in other art forms such as painting, children's culture and film. It provides a detailed analysis of magic realism in the painting of the Weimar Republic and how this form of painting has been associated with hyper-realist painters in North America in the second half of the twentieth century, such as Alex Colville and Edward Hopper. The painting of Frida Kahlo will also be examined as an example of cross-over art between European magic realism and the marvellous and magical realism of mid-twentieth century Latin America. This chapter will also consider the close relationship of magic and reality in children's culture and its similarities in attitudes to magical realist writing and film. In this chapter the magical realism of films such as Frank Capra's *It's a Wonderful Life* (1946), Wim Wender's *Wings of Desire* (1987) and Spike Jonze's *Being John Malkovich* (1999) will also be examined as a separate category from magical realist fiction in recognition of its relationship to both narrative fiction and pictorial art.

The final chapter brings together debates about the future and the appropriateness of magical realism in relation to postcolonialism and the cultural contexts in which these fictions are created. This chapter focuses on the problem that many readers of magical realism do not come from the same cultural context as that of the writer or of the text and therefore have a different understanding of what constitutes reality and the magical. In this chapter questions will be asked such as whether readers can really suspend their own judgements whilst reading a magical realist novel from another culture, and whether a Western reader can read and accept the opposing assumptions of a non-Western novel without reverting to assumptions about the superiority of their own Western and possibly colonialist perspective. Ultimately, this chapter will consider the future of magical realism and will attempt to assess the usefulness of the terms in relation to contemporary cultural production.

This book has been written in order to provide a guide to the range of ideas concerning magic(al) realism and to explain their relationship to each other, rather than to provide a limiting definition of the term. It also points to the ways in which magic(al) realism can be a highly appropriate and significant concept for cultural production created in the context of increasing heterogeneity and cross-culturalism at the end of the twentieth century and into the twenty-first.

1

ORIGINS OF MAGIC(AL) REALISM

The history of magic(al) realism, that is, of the related terms of magic realism, magical realism and marvellous realism, is a complicated story spanning eight decades with three principal turning points and many characters. The first period is set in Germany in the 1920s, the second period in Central America in the 1940s and the third period, beginning in 1955 in Latin America, continues internationally to this day. All these periods are linked by literary and artistic figures whose works spread the influence of magic(al) realism around Europe, from Europe to Latin America, and from Latin America to the rest of the world. The key figures in the development of the term are the German art critic Franz Roh best known for his work in the 1920s, the mid-twentieth-century Cuban writer Alejo Carpentier, the Italian writer Massimo Bontempelli from the 1920s and 1930s, the mid-twentieth-century Latin American literary critic Angel Flores and the late twentieth-century Latin American novelist Gabriel García Márquez.

Many people have been associated with the development of magic(al) realism in its recognized forms of post-expressionist painting from 1920s Germany and modernist and postmodernist modes of writing from Europe in the early twentieth century, and Latin America and the

English-speaking world in the second half of the twentieth century. Although it is now most famously associated with Latin America, many of its influences can be traced to European literature, particularly of the modernist period at the beginning of the twentieth century. Magic realist painting shares with modernism an attempt to find a new way of expressing a deeper understanding of reality witnessed by the artist and writer through experimentation with painting and narrative techniques. It, for instance, rejected previous styles to create a clarity and smoothness of the picture that was an amalgamation of the influences of photography and Renaissance art. Magic(al) realist writing, moreover, has become associated with the modernist techniques of the disruption of linear narrative time and the questioning of the notion of history.

Magic(al) realism is a contested term primarily because the majority of critics increase the confusion surrounding its history by basing their consideration of the term on one of its explanations rather than acknowledging the full complexity of its origins. For this reason the critic Roberto González Echevarría finds it difficult to validate a 'true history' of the concept (1977: 112). The American critic Seymour Menton is one of the few who do attempt to unravel its past. The Appendix to his book *Historia verdadera del realismo mágico* (The True History of Magic Realism) is a chronology of the term, and its sub-title reveals the irony of the book's title: Menton heads the Appendix with a series of queried dates that have all been claimed to be the original date of the coining of the term: '1925, 1924, 1923, 1922?' (1998: 209).

The consensus amongst the majority of contemporary critics, such as Amaryll Chanady, Seymour Menton, Lois Parkinson Zamora and Wendy Faris, is that the German art critic Franz Roh (1890–1965) introduced the term to refer to a new form of post-expressionist painting during the Weimar Republic. In his 1925 book *Nach-Expressionismus, Magischer Realismus: Probleme der neusten europäischen Malerei* (*Post-expressionism, Magic Realism: Problems of the Most Recent European Painting*) he coined the term that is translated as 'magic realism' to define a form of painting that differs greatly from its predecessor (expressionist art) in its attention to accurate detail, a smooth photograph-like clarity of picture and the representation of the mystical non-material aspects of reality. Roh identified more than fifteen painters active in Germany at his time of writing to exemplify the form, including Otto Dix, Max Ernst,

Alexander Kanoldt, George Grosz and Georg Schrimpf. Their paintings differ greatly from each other. Some magic realist paintings, such as those by Otto Dix and George Grosz, verge on grotesque caricature. The bodies of the subjects of their paintings are disproportionately small in comparison to their emphasized faces. In Otto Dix's *Match Seller I* (1920) an amputee with a face the size of his body and words written from his mouth cartoon-style sits on a pavement and is urinated on by a dog. George Grosz's *Gray Day* (1921) shows an impossibly round-headed businessman with crossed eyes traversing an industrial landscape in the opposite direction to a hunch-backed soldier with a large head and hands. Both painters show a disregard for traditional and realistic perspective. In *The Match Seller I* the passers-by appear to be falling over due to the strange angle at which their legs are painted while the soldier in *Gray Day* appears to be walking in mid-air due to the lack of perspective of the background walls and buildings. Other magic realist paintings, such as the calm, realistic still-lifes by Alexander Kanoldt, are less obviously 'magical'. They focus on traditional still-life subjects such as, for instance, a potted-palm tree on a side table next to a bottle and small tray in *Still Life II* (1926). All the objects are given equal importance in the composition. The focus of attention is drawn as much to the heavy backcloth as it is to the palm since both are depicted with similar depth of shading. The clarity of the objects in the picture and the lack of emphasis of any one object provide the distinctive 'magical' aspect of this painting. Yet to Roh the magical aspect of this art was not of a religious nor of the 'witch and wizard' kind but was the 'magic of being' which celebrated the 'world's rational organization' (Guenther 1995: 35). The art historian Irene Guenther succinctly notes: 'The juxtaposition of "magic" and "realism" reflected . . . the monstrous and marvellous *Unheimlichkeit* [uncanniness] within human beings and inherent in their modern technological sur-roundings' (1995: 36). This form of magic was partly influenced by the psychoanalytical writings of Sigmund Freud and by the earlier paintings of Giorgio de Chirico (1888–1978) of the Italian '*arte metafisica*' movement who shared with the German magic realists the severe repre-sentation of objects from unfamiliar angles (ibid.: 38). There are also claims by critics such as Jean Pierre Durix that the director of the Museum of Art in Mannheim in the early 1920s, G. F. Hartlaub, coined the term in relation to an exhibition of paintings by Max Beckmann that he organized in 1923 (1998: 103). However, as Hartlaub abandoned the term 'magic realism' in preference to *'neue Sachlichkeit'* (new objectivity) before an exhibition in 1926 of the same artists whom Roh identified as magic realists, the development of the term, if not the coining of it, appears to rest with Roh. Roh also abandoned the term several years later when he recognized that Hartlaub's term 'new objectivity' had endured longer and had more currency amongst the artistic community (Crockett 1999: 3). All things considered, despite the need felt by some critics to identify a specific originator of the term, the fact that the term was coined around the early 1920s in relation to a particular group of painters based in Germany, sharing a similar vision, is adequate to provide the necessary understanding of the context of its creation.

The historical context in which magic realist painting developed was that of the unstable German Weimar Republic during the period 1919–23. This era followed the German defeat in the First World War and the abdication and flight into exile of the Kaiser in 1918. It was a period of political fragility when the vacuum of power that was created following the abdication of the Kaiser was fought over by right-wing and left-wing revolutionary groups, including the National Socialist German Worker's Party of Adolf Hitler, founded in 1920. It was an era of political violence (the Minister for Reconstruction was assassinated in 1922) and extreme economic difficulty due to the destruction of the economy of Germany by the war and the demands for reparation by their victors (Davies 1996: 941–2). High inflation and separatist and revolutionary activity created national anxiety that was little tempered by the rule of a weak coalition government (Michalski 1994: 7). Democratically distanced from the rest of Europe and caught between the demolition of their old world and the uncertainty of the future, a desire for *'Sachlichkeit'* (matter-of-factness) was the growing focus of the nation (ibid.: 8). The art historian Sergiusz Michalski summarizes the mood of the time and its influence on magic realist painting in his thorough study of art in the Weimar Republic, stating: 'Ultimately, it was a reflection of German society at that time, torn between a desire for and simultaneous fear of unconditional modernity, between sober, objective rationality and residues of Expressionist and rationalist irrationalities' (ibid.: 13). The premise behind Roh's analytical and theoretical work on magic realism, with which he attempted to define the predominant art movement in the

Weimar Republic, was the need to identify one characteristic different from those of the influential movements of expressionism, such as the painting of Vincent Van Gogh, and surrealism, such as the painting of Salvador Dalí. In fact, he constructed a list of twenty-two characteristics that differentiated magic realism from expressionism in his 1925 book. These included the expressionist warmth of the colours and rough, thick texture of the paint surface, the emphasis of the painting process and the spontaneous effect of the expressionists as opposed to the smooth, carefully constructed, cool photographic quality of magic realist painting. Roh considered magic realism to be related to, but distinctive from, surrealism due to magic realism's focus on the material object and the actual existence of things in the world, as opposed to the more cerebral and psychological reality explored by the surrealists. These distinctions will be examined further in the following chapter in which magic realism is distinguished from other art movements and genres.

For Roh, the most important aspect of magic realist painting was that the mystery of the concrete object needed to be caught through painting realistically: 'the thing, the object, must be formed anew' (1995: 113). By doing so, Roh hoped to encourage the artist to take the psychoanalytical influences of Sigmund Freud and Carl Jung from surrealism and to combine them with an endeavour to represent the object clearly with all its 'wondrous meaning'. The surrealists had been greatly influenced by the revolutionary explorations of the human mind by Freud and Jung. Their explanations of the subconscious and unconscious mind's influence over the actions, thoughts and particularly the dreams of people had led the surrealists to consider the inadequacy of art that attempted to realistically present the exterior and material world without expressing the influence of the inner-life on it. Freud's work on the interpretation of dreams, published at the turn of the century, had a particularly strong influence on the surrealists. In his study of surrealism Wallace Fowlie explains that, following the influence of Freud and Jung on them, the surrealists considered that 'conscious states of man's being are not sufficient to explain him to himself and others' (1960: 16). For Roh, magic realist painting needed to incorporate these ideas about the interior life of humans into painting whilst expressing it through depictions of the material world. Roh considered the mystery of life and the complexities of the inner-life of humans to be perceivable through the close observation of objects. He called on artists to act upon his discovery that 'For the new art, it is a question of representing before our eyes, in an intuitive way, *the fact, the interior figure, of the exterior world*' (Roh 1995: 24).

Much of the confusion concerning magic realism arises from the fact that it was contemporary with surrealism. Surrealist manifestos were written in 1924 and 1930, and some claim it is a branch of this art movement. There are similarities between the two movements, and it is important to note that at a later date magic(al) realist writers, particularly Alejo Carpentier, were influenced by both Roh and the surrealists. The similarities are significant, not least the surrealists' desire to draw out the hidden psychic aspects of life into art, their desire for newness following war, and their attempts to harmonize contradictions and paradoxes. These will be discussed in more detail in the next chapter. However, the theorists of both surrealism and Roh's magic realism emphasized the differences of their artistic movements in an attempt to define them as distinct.

This initial form of magic realist painting was not confined to Germany: its influence spread so that similar images could be seen in France, Holland and Italy. Later still, following the influence of an exhibition of art by German magic realist painters in New York in 1931, an exhibition called 'American Realists and Magic Realists' (1943) even identified the hyper-realist American painter Edward Hopper (1882–1967) who is famous for his smooth and photographic style and quiet, city-scapes, as an exponent of magic realist art (Menton 1998: 219–220).

The influence of Roh's term 'magic realism' and its theoretical implications had even greater influence than that of the painting, with two particularly notable consequences. First, the Italian writer Massimo Bontempelli (1878–1960), influenced initially by surrealism and then by German magic realism at the time of Mussolini's fascist rule in Italy, founded the bilingual magazine *900.Novecento* in 1926. It was written in French and Italian and published magic realist writing and criticism (Menton 1998: 212). His idea of magic realism coincided for the most part with that of Roh; Robert Dombroski in *The Cambridge History of Italian Literature* notes that Bontempelli sought to present 'the mysterious and fantastic quality of reality' (1996: 522). He differed from Roh in that he applied these thoughts to writing and not to pictorial art. Also, Bontempelli was influenced by fascism and wanted magic realist writing to provide means to inspire the Italian nation and to make Italian culture more international in outlook. As Dombroski notes, he defined the function of literature as a means to create a collective consciousness by 'opening new mythical and magical perspectives on reality' (1996: 522). His writing was sometimes more fantastical than magic(al) realist and was often close to the surreal, but he has been cited as the first magic realist creative writer, and the fact that his magazine was bilingual meant that its influence was Europe-wide. For instance, his work influenced the Flemish writers Johan Daisne and Hubert Lampo in post-Second World War Flanders during the 1940s and 1950s to adopt the magic realist mode (Lampo 1993: 33).

The second significant influence of the term is the most widely recognized development in magic(al) realism; the influence of Roh's work in Latin America. In 1927, the chapters specifically concerning magic realism from Franz Roh's *Nach-Expressionismus, Magischer Realismus* were translated into Spanish by Fernando Vela and published in Madrid by *Revista de Occidente* under the title *Realismo mágico. Post-expresionismo: Problemas de la pintura europea mas reciente.* The publications of *Revista de Occidente* were widely circulated amongst writers in Latin America such as Miguel Angel Asturias and Jorge Luis Borges and have been acknowledged to have had a far-reaching influence, particularly as they provided many first translations of important European texts for the Latin American readership (Menton 1998: 214).

As well as Roh's influence, another important thread in the development of magic(al) realism can be traced from post-expressionist and surrealist Europe to Latin America. Two diplomats and writers, a French-Russian Cuban, Alejo Carpentier (1904–80), and Venezuelan Arturo Uslar-Pietri (1906–2001), were strongly influenced by European artistic movements while living in Paris in the 1920s and 1930s. It is Carpentier who, having immersed himself in European art and literature in the 1920s, has become most widely acknowledged as the originator of Latin American magic(al) realism. After returning from Europe to Cuba and having travelled in Haiti, he instigated a distinctly Latin American form of magic realism, coining the phrase '*lo realismo maravilloso*' (marvellous realism) (Echevarría 1977: 97). Having been witness to European surrealism, he recognized a need for art to express the non-material aspects of life but also recognized the differences between his European and his Latin American contexts. He used the term 'marvellous realism' to describe a concept that could represent for him the mixture of differing cultural systems and the variety of experiences that create an extraordinary atmosphere, alternative attitude and differing appreciation of reality in Latin America.

The idea of the unique and extraordinary reality of Latin America was not a new concept. The Spanish 'conqueror' of Mexico, Hernando Cortés, in the sixteenth century reported being unable to describe in familiar European terms what he saw on the American continents. However, Carpentier saw the unique aspects of Latin America in its racial and cultural mixture rather than in the flora and fauna. He first considered these ideas in an essay he wrote for the widely read Venezuelan publication *El Nacional* and more famously expanded his theory of Latin American reality in the prologue to his 1949 novel *El reino de este mundo* (*The Kingdom of this World*). In this prologue, while dis-associating himself and his writing from Roh's magic realism on the grounds of its cold artificiality and 'tiresome pretension' (Carpentier 1995a: 84), he proposed marvellous reality to be 'the heritage of all of America' (ibid.: 87). In the introduction to his prologue, translated into English and reproduced in their book *Magical Realism: Theory, History, Community* (1995), Lois Parkinson Zamora and Wendy Faris explain that in Carpentier's terms, as opposed to the surrealists, 'improbable juxta-positions and marvellous mixtures exist by virtue of Latin America's varied history, geography, demography, and politics – not by manifesto' (75).

Arturo Uslar-Pietri, who influenced fellow Venezuelan writers with his magic realist short stories during the 1930s and 1940s, was most closely associated with Franz Roh's form of post-expressionist 'magic realism' and had known Bontempelli in Paris (Guenther 1995: 61). His writing emphasized the mystery of human living amongst the reality of life rather than following Carpentier's newly developing versions of marvellous American reality. He considered magic realism to be a continuation of the '*vanguardia*' modernist experimental writings of Latin America. Because of his close association with modernism and the original ideas of Franz Roh, some critics such as Maria Elena Angulo stress Uslar-Pietri's role in bringing magic realism to Latin America before Alejo Carpentier (1995: 1). However, the majority of critics recognize the fiction of Carpentier to

be amongst the most influential magic(al) realist writing while Uslar-
Pietri's work remains largely unknown outside Spanish-speaking Latin
America. Ultimately, it has been Carpentier and not Uslar-Pietri who is
predominantly remembered for bringing magic realism to the continent,
for producing the specifically Latin American form of marvellous realism.
It is his work that has been cited as an influence on the writing of such
important magical realists as Gabriel García Márquez, whose work has
come to epitomize Latin American writing in the latter half of the
twentieth century.

The return of Carpentier and Uslar-Pietri to Latin America coincided
with a large migration of Europeans, particularly from Spain, looking
for a new start following the Second World War and the fall of the
Spanish Republic. The 1940s also became a time of maturation for many
Latin American countries and consequently they sought to create and
express a consciousness distinct from that of Europe (Echevarría 1977:
99). In Cuba, Carpentier was at the forefront of such a movement and
was commissioned to write books such as a history of Cuban music (ibid.:
101). As Echevarría notes, 'Carpentier's artistic enterprise in the forties
became a search for origins, the recovery of history and tradition, the
foundation of an autonomous American consciousness serving as the basis
for a literature faithful to the New World' (ibid.: 107).

While both magic realism and marvellous realism refer to distinct
and different versions of magic(al) realism, a new term 'magical realism'
has emerged in criticism following the 1955 essay 'Magical Realism in
Spanish American Fiction' by the critic Angel Flores. This term can be
used to refer to the versions of magic(al) realism that have aspects of
both magic realism and marvellous realism. Later chapters will consider
the differences whereby magic realism is related to art forms reaching
for a new clarity of reality, and marvellous realism refers to a concept
representing the mixture of differing world views and approaches to what
constitutes reality. Naming Jorge Luis Borges (1899–1986) as the first
magical realist, Flores recounts both European modernist and specifically
Spanish influences for this version of magic(al) realism. Controversially,
he does not acknowledge either Uslar-Pietri or Carpentier for bringing
Roh's magic realism to Latin America and instead argues that magical
realism is a continuation of the romantic realist tradition of Spanish
language literature and its European counterparts. For this purpose, Flores

created a new history of influences on the production of Latin American magical realism that could be traced back to the sixteenth century Spanish writer Miguel de Saavedra Cervantes, the turn of the twentieth century Czech-Austrian writer Franz Kafka and also (sharing some influences with Roh) European modernists such as the Italian painter Giorgio de Chirico (1995: 112). Although written over three hundred years earlier, Cervantes' novel *Don Quixote* is often thought of as a precursor to magical realism. *The Dictionary of the Literature of the Iberian Peninsula* explains the dynamic in the novel that makes it compatible with the idea of magical realism: 'The opposition between the mad, book-inspired, idealistic knight and his sane, pragmatic, materialistic squire appears to be absoluted at the beginning of their relationship' (Bleiberg *et al.* 1993: 383). Most famously, the knight Don Quixote battles with windmills believing them to be knights he must fight. For his version of magical realism, Flores drew on the interpretation that Don Quixote's belief in what he perceives is absolute but can be seen by his companion, the squire Sancho Panza, and the reader differently. Flores was inspired by Kafka's most famous tale 'Metamorphosis', a realist story of a man who wakes up to find that he has become an insect and continues to live with his family, adjusting his life to his new circumstances as if it were an unalterable part of reality. The painter Giorgio de Chirico was considered by Flores to be the precursor to the magic realist painters of Germany, who were influenced by his cold, smooth style depicting empty and immense man-made industrial landscapes.

Jorge Luis Borges himself is often thought of as the father of modern Latin American writing and a precursor to magical realism. He is only considered to be a true magical realist by Angel Flores who emphasizes the influence of Borges to the extent of claiming that his 1935 collection of short fiction *Historia universal de la infamia* (*A Universal History of Infamy*) was the first example of Latin American magical realist writing (Flores 1995: 113). Borges was the perfect example of Flores' theory that magical realism was influenced by European literature. Borges had previously written a manifesto introducing modernist literary techniques to Argentina in 1921 (Verani 1996: 122). While living in Spain, he had been influenced by the '*Ultraísmo*' movement, which was the main form of modernist experimentalism in Spain. The movement adopted minimalist poetic techniques to create poetry that was stripped down to almost unconnected metaphors lacking in ornamentation and sentimentality and Borges wanted to introduce such techniques to Latin America (Lindstrom 1994: 65). He had been strongly influenced additionally by the writer Kafka, whose realist writing which verged on surrealism he had anthologized and translated into Spanish (Flores 1995: 113). Despite the lack of a direct acknowledgement by Borges of Roh's influence on his work, it is considered probable that Borges had knowledge of Roh's ideas when he wrote his influential essay '*El arte narrativo y la magia*' (Narrative Art and Magic) in 1932. For these reasons, he is often seen as the predecessor of current-day magical realists, gleaning influences from both European and Latin American cultural movements. The mixture of cultural influences has remained a key aspect of magical realist writing.

Following the publication of Flores' essay there was renewed interest in Latin America in Carpentier and his form of marvellous realism. The combination of these influences led to the second wave of magic(al) realist writing which is best known as 'magical realism' but which is not directly associated with the definition of the term as outlined by Angel Flores except that it does combine elements of both marvellous realism and magic realism. It is most notable for its matter-of-fact depiction of magical happenings. It developed into one of the most recognizable types of Latin American literature today having emerged following the success of the Cuban revolution in 1959. With a sense of euphoria and the search for new beginnings for Latin America, there was a cultural wave of creativity and in particular a 'boom' of writing that sought to produce modern and specifically Latin American fiction (Pope 1996: 226). Many writers set their work in Latin America whilst importing European modernist literary techniques. For instance, whilst writing recognizably Latin American fiction, García Márquez lists Kafka and James Joyce amongst his other influences (Connell 1998: 98).

The international recognition of Latin American magic(al) realists such as Carpentier and most particularly García Márquez has led to a misconceived assumption that magic(al) realism is specifically Latin American. This ignores both the Latin American connections of early twentieth-century European art and literature and the very different related German art movement known as 'magic realism' with its influences within Europe. Yet, the fame of Latin American magical realism has propelled the rapid adoption of this form of writing globally. Magical realist writers have become recognized in India, Canada, Africa, the United States and across the world. Most famously, Salman Rushdie has been influenced by both the magical realism of García Márquez and the German magic realism of Günter Grass. The traces of these influences indicate the complexity and inter-relatedness of the various off-shoots of magic(al) realism. This will be discussed in more detail in Chapter 3.

All magic(al) realist writers have their own influences, some from contemporary writers, some stretching back to the origins of the term and some from before the term was coined. Whatever the influences, it is rare for a writer to be concerned with questions such as the origin of the critical term. However, whilst discussing the term in critical practice it is important to understand the context of the developments of the term and the varieties covered by it. This chapter has sketched the development of the related terms, and the following chapter will consider how to differentiate these terms from each other, from their influences and from other apparently similar forms.

2

DELIMITING THE TERMS

Magic realism, magical realism and marvellous realism are highly disputed terms, not only due to their complicated history but also because they encompass many variants. Their wide scope means that they often appear to encroach on other genres and terms. Therefore, one of the best ways of reaching some form of definition is to establish to what they are related, and to what they are not related. In this chapter I will be delimiting the terms magic and magical realism (sometimes encapsulating both in the term magic(al) realism) by examining their relationships to other genres and terms such as realism, surrealism, allegory and the fantastic. As these terms and the critics referred to in this chapter are literary, I will consider magical realism solely in relation to narrative fiction. As there is also a need to delimit magic realist painting from other artistic movements, there is a study of magic realist art in Chapter 6.

It follows that a definition of magic(al) realism relies upon the prior understanding of what is meant by 'magic' and what is meant by 'realism'. 'Magic' is the less theorized term of the two, and contributes to the variety of definitions of magic(al) realism. In fact, each of the versions of magic(al) realism have differing meanings for the term 'magic'; in magic realism 'magic' refers to the mystery of life: in marvellous and magical realism 'magic' refers to any extraordinary occurrence and particularly to anything spiritual or unaccountable by rational science. The variety of magical occurrences in magic(al) realist writing includes ghosts, disappearances, miracles, extraordinary talents and strange atmospheres but does not include the magic as it is found in a magic show. Conjuring 'magic' is brought about by tricks that give the illusion that something extraordinary has happened, whereas in magic(al) realism it is assumed that something extraordinary *really* has happened.

When referring to magical realism as a narrative mode, it is essential to consider the relationship of 'magical' to 'realism' as it is understood in literary terms. 'Realism' is a much contested term, and none more so than when used in attempting to define magical realism. The term itself came into being through philosophical discussion in the mid-eighteenth century but is related to the ancient Greek philosopher Aristotle's concept of mimesis. Realism as a term in relation to art and literature only came into common use in the mid-nineteenth century but has since become widely recognized. The critic Ian Watt explains the philosophical notion that 'Modern realism . . . begins from the position that truth can be discovered by the individual through his sense: it has origins in Descartes and Locke' (1992: 89). By accepting that there is a reliable link between our senses and the world in which we live, realism assumes that 'the external world is real, and that our senses give us a true report of it' (Watt 1992: 89). The idea of portraying real actions in art was first discussed by Aristotle who claimed that the act of imitating life, or mimesis, is a natural instinct of humans. Aristotle explains the ancient Greek belief that witnessing art is an essential way to learn about the universal truths of life. For this the art itself must appear to be real to the reader or viewer in depicting something that exists, has existed or could or should exist. In fact, Aristotle paved the way for what we now understand of the realism of fictional narratives. He claimed that it is better to convince the reader of the realism of something impossible rather than to be unconvincing about something that is true (Aristotle 1920: 91).

Realism is most often associated with the tradition of the novel as its expansive form, in contrast to shorter fiction, allows the writer to present many details that contribute to a realistic impression. The tradition of the novel has developed as a predominantly realistic form with notable deviations (such as the romance, the modernist or the magical realist novel). Late nineteenth- and early twentieth-century novelists such as Henry James wrote essays discussing this relationship between the novel and reality. James claimed 'The only reason for the existence of the novel is that it does attempt to represent life' ([1934] 1992: 43). His advice on novel writing was to create as realistic a version of recognizable life as possible in order to engage the interest and sympathy of the reader: 'The characters, the situation, which strike one as real will be those that touch and interest one most' (James 1992: 43). Catherine Belsey, calling this 'Classical Realism' notes that in the late nineteenth century the novel was expected to 'show' rather than 'tell' the reader an interpretation of reality (1980: 68).

However, twentieth century theories of realism in literature, including those by Henry James, emphasize the involvement of the imaginative process in literature so that, as David Grant explains, 'Here realism is achieved not by imitation, but by creation; a creation which, working with the raw materials of life, absolves these by the intercession of the imagination from mere factuality and translates them to a higher order' (1970: 15). In this understanding of realism it is the reader who constructs the sense of reality from the narrative rather than the text revealing the author's interpretation of reality to the reader. Importantly, as Watt notes, this form of realism emphasizes the importance of the narrative: 'the novel's realism does not reside in the kind of life it presents, but in the way it presents it' (1992: 89). In this sense, as Catherine Belsey notes, the way in which the narrative is constructed is a key element to the construction of twentieth-century realism. She explains that: 'Realism is plausible not because it reflects the world, but because it is constructed out of what is (discursively) familiar' (1980: 47). This approach to literary realism is the most relevant to magical realism, as magical realism relies upon the presentation of real, imagined or magical elements as if they were real. The key to understanding how magical realism works is to understand the way in which the narrative is constructed in order to provide a realistic context for the magical events of the fiction. Magical realism therefore relies upon realism but only so that it can stretch what is acceptable as real to its limits. It is therefore related to realism but is a narrative mode distinct from it.

Surrealism is another genre that is related to realism, as is indicated in its name, and it is often confused with magic(al) realism. In the previous chapter, I noted the historical connection of Franz Roh's notion of magic realism to surrealism, and the resulting influence on Alejo Carpentier's

Latin American marvellous realism. However, it is imperative in understanding the variants of magic(al) realism to be able to distinguish early
magic realism and its close relationship with surrealism from the
contemporary narrative mode of magical realism which has no connection
with surrealism.

Whilst both magic realism and surrealism in their most limited
definitions are movements of literature and art that developed in the first
half of the twentieth century, both terms have life beyond this period
as more generally applied notions. It is as common to hear someone say
'How surreal!' as it is to see a book described as magic realist on its dust
cover. Both surrealist and magic(al) realist writing and art could be called
revolutionary in their attitudes since surrealists attempted to write against
realist literature that reflected and reinforced what they considered to be
bourgeois society's idea of itself, and magic(al) realism holds immense
political possibilities in its disruption of categories. Although there are
debates about what surrealism means, it is often confused with magical
realism as it explores the non-pragmatic, non-realist aspects of human
existence. Consider, for instance, Salvador Dalí's painting *The Persistence
of Memory* (1931). This painting is surrealist because it attempts to
portray an aspect of life, memory, that is psychological yet attempts to
do so through pictoral and therefore physical means. The setting of the
painting that portrays Dalí's famous 'soft watches' is a landscape that
has familiar elements but that is unreal in its overall composition. The
watches are very clearly depicted and yet are extraordinary in that they
have insects on them and are malformed. They appear to be paradoxically
made from metal and yet are as flexible as fabric. Typical of surrealism, all
of the elements of the painting are familiar in themselves and yet are
distorted or placed out of context in order to express a non-physical aspect
of life. This painting exemplifies those aspects of surrealism that appear
to be similar to magical realism, such as the reliance of surrealism on
contradiction and the unifying of paradoxes. It could be said that the
premise of magical realism – to bring together the aspects of the real and
the magical – is in accordance with this aspect of surrealism, as magical
realism is such a paradox that is unified by the creation of a narrative in
which magic is incorporated seamlessly into reality. However, Dalí's
painting also reveals the relationship of surrealism with the psychological
and the unreal that distinguishes it from magical realism.

Surrealism is most distinct from magical realism since the aspects that it explores are associated not with material reality but with the imagination and the mind, and in particular it attempts to express the 'inner life' and psychology of humans through art. The critic Wallace Fowlie explains that the surrealists considered that 'conscious states of man's being are not sufficient to explain him to himself and others' (1960: 16) and therefore sought to express the sub-conscious and the unconscious. The extraordinary in magical realism is rarely presented in the form of a dream or a psychological experience because to do so takes the magic out of recognizable material reality and places it into the little understood world of the imagination. The ordinariness of magical realism's magic relies on its accepted and unquestioned position in tangible and material reality.

In addition, surrealism has been identified as an artistic movement that lasted from 1919 to 1939 and that was defined by its practitioners through a manifesto. Magic(al) realism in any of its variants has been discussed and nuanced by many critics and writers but has never been ultimately defined in this way. If we take our basic definition of magical realism established in the Introduction and compare it with the manifesto of surrealism written in 1924 by the French writer and most famous literary surrealist André Breton (1896–1966), we can see that there are clear differences. As with any movement defined by a manifesto, the absolute nature of its statements reveals a certainty concerning the term, which is lacking in magical realist criticism. Take for instance the very specific and certain surrealist statement that the psychic upheaval of war is rejuvenating in its persuasion of the new generation to break from the old and seek new ways of thinking. There is no such specific political or thematic definition of magical realism. Likewise, André Breton promoted the idea that we need to emphasize the 'savage' aspects of humans that are suppressed by the social order. These types of comments have little to do with magical realism, as magical realism relies upon a lack of judgement and distinction between what is 'savage', 'primitive' or sophisticated.

The magic(al) realist critic Amaryll Chanady has also carried out a study, *Magical Realism and the Fantastic: Resolved Versus Unresolved Antinomy*, in which she compares magical realism and surrealism, but her distinctions rely upon a definition of magical realism that she limits to Latin America: 'The difference is that the irrational world view in one [magical realism] represents the primitive American mentality, while in the other [surrealism], it corresponds to European superstitions' (1985: 21). What she is actually recognizing is Alejo Carpentier's distinction between European and Latin American magic realism. She summarizes this idea stating, 'While magic realism is based on an ordered, even if irrational, perspective, surrealism brings about "artificial" combinations' (Chanady 1985: 21).

Another term that is frequently associated with magic(al) realism is that of the fantastic. It is often erroneously assumed that magic realism and magical realism are forms of fantastical writing. When critics discuss magical realist novels such as Salman Rushdie's *Midnight's Children* ([1981] 1982) in terms of the fantastic, their approach to these texts provides them with very different interpretations to those by magical realist critics. Neil Cornwell's 1990 study *The Literary Fantastic: From Gothic to Postmodernism* analyses magical realist novels by Rushdie and Toni Morrison as examples of the genre of the fantastic. By doing so he assumes that the existence of a baby ghost in Morrison's *Beloved*, or the narrator vanishing into thin air inside a wicker basket thanks to a magic spell in Rushdie's *Midnight's Children* are presented by the narrators to be extraordinary events within a realist tale. A magical realist interpretation considers these two elements to be presented by the narrator to the reader as ordinary events in a realist story. These different interpretations occur because of the ambiguity of the novels themselves. For instance, Rushdie's narrator, Saleem, tells his friend Padma that she can 'believe, don't believe' but that 'magic spells can occasionally succeed' (Rushdie 1982: 381). Padma has doubts about his story but for Saleem he is telling the real story of his life.

These differing interpretations of the same novel exemplify the subtlety of the distinction between the two terms. Chanady explores this problem in her study of magical realism and the fantastic, in which she follows the majority of critics who adopt the seminal definition of the fantastic by the contemporary theorist and critic Tzvetan Todorov. Todorov defines fantastic literature as a piece of narrative in which there is a constant faltering between belief and non-belief in the supernatural or extraordinary event presented. For Todorov, the fantastic relies upon the reader's hesitation between natural and supernatural explanations for the fictional events in the text. This may be a hesitation that is shared with a character in the novel, or it may be emphasized in the text to produce a theme of ambiguity and hesitation (Todorov 1975: 25). He refers to Henry James' 'The Turn of the Screw' ([1898] 1986) as a clear example of fantastic literature (Todorov 1975: 43). In this short story a governess finds herself left alone in a house with an unsympathetic housekeeper and the children in her care who tell her about the ghosts that they see. The governess becomes increasingly afraid and embroiled in her wariness of the ghosts. The story is told from the governess's perspective to give the impression to the reader that the ghosts do indeed exist but there is adequate additional comment to suggest that she may in fact be delusional, and even perhaps simply attention-seeking. This element of doubt and the governess's own fear of the unknown, of the supernatural, stops the text from being magical realist, but it is exactly this hesitation between the two explanations – there are really ghosts or she is really mad – that affirms its fantastical nature.

Neil Cornwell's analysis of Rushdie and Morrison as fantastical writers goes against the idea prevalent in magical realist criticism that the narrator and reader accept the existence of the magical elements in the text. Chanady pinpoints this difference between the fantastic and the magical realist:

> In contrast to the fantastic, the supernatural in magical realism does not disconcert the reader, and this is the fundamental difference between the two modes. The same phenomena that are portrayed as problematical by the author of a fantastic narrative are presented in a matter-of-fact manner by the magical realist.
>
> (1985: 24)

While this is a workable way to delimit magical realism from its close relations, it does need careful consideration. For instance, there is confusion concerning Kafka. He is well known as a primary influence on magical realist writers, but he is not usually considered to be a magical realist writer himself. Despite this, Chanady applies her definition of magical realism to Kafka's short story 'Metamorphosis' ([1915] 1961). She claims that, as Georg Samsa wakes up and finds himself to be an insect and does not seek an explanation for what has happened to him, he is expressing his condition in a matter-of-fact magical realist manner.

However, if one looks more closely, one realizes that Georg is afraid to admit to his family what has happened to him, and his family are shocked upon discovering him. Whilst he considers it to be his fate, he does not consider his condition to be a part of what he previously recognized as everyday reality. In fact, the tragic ending, when he is killed by his own family, is rather more an affirmation of his and his family's rejection of the extraordinariness. What this illustrates is that it is possible to have magical realist elements in a text that is not consistently magical realist in its approach. However, unless the magical aspects are accepted as part of everyday reality throughout the text, the text cannot be called magical realist.

A further complication in identifying Kakfa's writing as magic realist, aside from the fact that he was writing in the 1910s well before Roh's coining of the term, is that his writing is often considered to be allegoric. According to *The Cambridge Guide to Literature in English*, allegory is the 'descriptive or narrative . . . presentation of literal characters and events which contain sustained reference to a simultaneous structure of other ideas and events' (Ousby 1993: 15–16). It is a narrative that has at least two levels of meaning. On one level the narrative makes sense as a plot. On another level, there is an alternative meaning to the plot which is often more philosophically profound than the plot itself. An often cited example of allegory is *Gulliver's Travels* ([1726] 1967) by Jonathan Swift. The plot suggests that the book is about a man who travels through extraordinary lands and recounts his experiences to his doubting fellow men on his return. However, the book can also be read as a comparative criticism of the ways human beings react to each other and other animals. In allegorical writing, the plot tends to be less significant than the alternative meaning in a reader's interpretation. This makes it difficult to incorporate allegory into a magical realist novel, as the importance of the alternative meaning interferes with the need for the reader to accept the reality of the magical aspects of the plot.

Tzvetan Todorov considers allegory to be incompatible with fantasy, as the allegorical meaning disturbs the tension between the fantastical and realistic elements. This is where other contemporary critics of the fantastic vary from Todorov's view. Neil Cornwell, for instance, whilst discussing Rushdie's *The Satanic Verses* ([1988] 1992) as fantastic literature, identifies the novel as a form of allegory. Cornwell claims that *The Satanic Verses* can be read as an allegory concerning its call for a new interpretation of Islam. He illustrates his argument, which is well supported by the text, by identifying the main characters Gibreel and Saladin, who fall from an airplane on their approach to London at the beginning of the novel, as the equivalents of the angel Gabriel and Satan. Rushdie reinforces the religious allegory by placing himself in the text in the guise of Salman the Persian, a scribe who notes down the new scriptures. The *fatwa* proclaimed against Rushdie for writing *The Satanic Verses* relied upon this religious allegorical interpretation of the book.

Many of Rushdie's works, whilst normally considered to be magical realist, are acknowledged to contain allegorical representations of particular political significance. The story of the narrator of *Midnight's Children*, Saleem, is an allegorical history of India's first thirty years after independence. Saleem is born at the moment that India becomes independent from colonial Britain. He has the gift to speak in his head to all the other similarly gifted children born at the same time as him in India and together they represent an enormous promise for a democratic and successful nation. However, by the end of the novel, like India losing its optimism for its future, the children have lost their gifts and Saleem feels himself to be disintegrating while India itself is dividing into factions. Although the novel *Midnight's Children* can be read as an allegory of the history of India this does not undermine the vivid presentation of the real and the magical in the narrative. For Rushdie's narrator, simply turning back in time and telling his story and the story of India is a magical act in itself: 'I was heading abracadabra abracadabra into the heart of a nostalgia which would keep me alive long enough to write these pages' (1982: 450). In this novel, the magical aspects of the narrative are essential to portray both the plot and the allegory.

Although we have seen Amaryll Chanady's convincing argument for not accepting magical realist novels as fantastical, critics who interpret magical realist novels under the umbrella of different terms or genres are not always mistaken. Allegory in Rushdie's work provides a perfect example of this type of delicate balance of identification. It is a question of the extent to which the allegorical meaning overshadows the realism of the plot. In fact, it is useful to consider the allegorical novel *Gulliver's Travels* in order to distinguish those aspects that limit the extent to which magical realism can also be allegorical. In his study of satire Arthur Pollard takes Jonathan Swift's *Gulliver's Travels* as the epitome of a satiric allegory (1970: 36). We can see that *Gulliver's Travels* is on the surface a story about a man who visits extraordinary places. However, the commentary on and the portrayal of his journey provide us with another level of meaning; the extraordinary lands that he visits are compared with Gulliver's own home and the reader is able shape his or her own criticisms of human life in comparison to those of the giants and other creatures that Gulliver visits. In this case the plot is overshadowed by the alternative meaning. Gulliver's narratives of his travels are read with irony because the reader simultaneously interprets the plot in relation to the criticism of human beings that Gulliver instigates. If we consider a magical realist narrative, we can see that it is problematic for it to have an alternate meaning that colours with irony the one presented on the surface. This comes close to the idea of a fable in which the story is told simply for its moral and the autonomy of the content of the narrative is dismissed. This undermines the claim on the realism of what is presented in the surface meaning, and most particularly undermines the attempt to present magical aspects as real.

Many of the problems of definition arise because of the frequent difficulty of placing texts into narrowly defined genres and categories. Kafka's 'Metamorphosis' is the perfect example of this. I have presented the arguments for considering aspects of it to be magical realist and allegorical. In his 2000 guide to science fiction, Adam Roberts notes that Kafka has even been described as a science fiction writer. These interpretations focus on differing aspects of the text: the allegorical interpretation focuses on Kafka's implied criticism of the way in which men are dehumanized in the capitalist system; the magical realist interpretation focuses on the realist narrative of a man turning into an insect; and the science fiction interpretation focuses on the event of a human metamorphosing into an insect. That it is possible for these critics to make such varied interpretations suggests that there is a closeness between magical realism, the fantastic, allegory and science fiction.

Many people assume that science fiction is a form of fantasy fiction involving things to do with space and the future. However, science fiction is as difficult a term as magical realism, so to provide an adequate distinction between the two forms relies upon a certain degree of acknowledgement of the slipperiness of the modes and their terms and definitions.

One of the characteristics of science fiction that distinguishes it from magical realism is its requirement of a rational, physical explanation for any unusual occurrence. Roberts refers to the work of Darko Suvin who uses the term 'novum' to express the thing or things which appear in a science fiction novel indicating that it is different from our own known world, but those things are explicable within or by extension of known science. One such science fiction novel that does not deal with the far-off future and is littered with nova (such as the soma drug, brain-washing and controlled reproduction) is Aldous Huxley's *Brave New World* ([1932] 1952). In this novel Huxley portrays a dystopian totalitarian world in which the population is highly controlled by mood enhancing drugs and a policed class system. In this world there is no link between sexual activity and reproduction. Babies are produced in laboratories where their abilities are chemically altered in accordance with their class. The science fiction narrative's distinct difference from magical realism is that it is set in a world different from any known reality and its realism resides in the fact that we can recognize it as a possibility for our future. Unlike magical realism, it does not have a realistic setting that is recognizable in relation to any past or present reality.

Like magical realism, science fiction is also associated with different genres and terms. Most particularly, Roberts points to the work of critic Robert Scholes who claims that science fiction is in fact a specific form of fable. Scholes explains that fable is 'fiction that offers us a world clearly and radically discontinuous from the one we know, yet returns to confront that known world in some cognitive way' (Roberts 2000: 10). Here Huxley's text can be seen to be a form of fable as a warning to the reader not to allow such a world to develop in reality.

The example of Huxley's *Brave New World* read as a fable illustrates the difference between science fiction as a form and magical realism. A magical realist novel may have important things to relate to the reader about their actual world, but the plot is not structured around this one message as it is in a fable. If we consider, for instance, 'The Pardoner's Tale' from Geoffrey Chaucer's *The Canterbury Tales* ([1387] 1974), we see that the narrator, the Pardoner, attempts to create a realistic setting for his tale, in an inn with three reprehensible young men. His tale, however, describes in a matter-of-fact tone how the figure of Death meets each of the three men with terrible consequences. This could be considered to be a magical realist narrative except for the fact that the narratorial voice of the Pardoner makes it clear that the tale is a fable from which the listener or reader should learn rather than a presentation of real events. The structure of the story is designed to deliver the moral and this undermines the realism of the plot, which is needed to support the possibility of the magical occurrences.

One further form of writing which could be confused with magical realism is the new journalistic writing of the 1970s and 1980s. While writing in a highly realistic style on the verge of journalistic factual reporting, writers such as Hunter S. Thompson produced books filled with accurate detail such as *Fear and Loathing in Las Vegas* ([1971] 1993), which follows a line of real investigation in recognizable locations whilst taking hallucinogenic drugs. As the narrator explains, 'Hallucinations are bad enough. But after a while you learn to cope with things like seeing your dead grandmother crawling up your leg with a knife in her teeth' (Thompson 1993: 47). The narratorial effect is indeed a mixture of the real and hallucination in a way that accepts the imaginary as an ordinary part of the reality. The reader and narrator, however, know that these imaginings are just that, originating from the mind and not present in the material world of recognizable reality.

These comments on the writing of Hunter S. Thompson when added to the distinctions made between magic(al) realism and realism, surrealism, the fantastical, allegory and science fiction, go to the heart of a working definition of narrative magical realism. Not only must the narrator propose real and magical happenings with the same matter-of-fact manner in a recognizably realistic setting but the magical things must be accepted as a part of material reality, whether seen or unseen. They cannot be simply the imaginings of one mind, whether under the influence of drugs, or for the purpose of exploring the workings of the mind, imagining our futures, or for making a moral point.

3

LOCATIONS OF MAGIC(AL) REALISM

To suggest that magic(al) realist writing can be found only in particular 'locations' would be misleading. It is after all a narrative mode, or a way of thinking in its most expansive form, and those concepts cannot be 'kept' in a geographic location. However, it is true to say that certain locations and countries have become associated with producing magic realist, and later magical realist writing. It has been noted that magical realist fictions are often set in rural areas away from influence over, or influence from, the political power centres. The Colombian novelist Gabriel García Márquez sets the majority of his novels in a fictional town called Macondo on the isolated Caribbean coast of Colombia. The African American novelist Toni Morrison, whilst sometimes setting her novels in the city, sets the magical realist events in rural areas and small townships. However, this is not the case for all magical realist texts, as some highly politically motivated writers have set their magical realist fictions in large cities that are the focus of political and social tensions. The British Indian writer Salman Rushdie, whose fictions are set in some of the world's largest urban areas such as London, Bombay or New York, is the most notable of these writers. However, each of these novels is portrayed from the marginal perspectives of people lacking political power, whether they are an impotent writer in a pickle factory in Bombay, or a group of young British Asian revolutionaries in London. For these reasons magical realism has become associated with fictions that tell the tales of those on the margins of political power and influential society. This has meant that much magical realism has originated in many of the postcolonial countries that are battling against the influence of their previous colonial rulers, and consider themselves to be at the margins of imperial power. It has also become a common narrative mode for fictions written from the perspective of the politically or culturally disempowered, for instance indigenous people living under a covert colonial system such as Native Americans in the United States, women writing from a feminist perspective, or those whose lives incorporate different cultural beliefs and practices from those dominant in their country of residence, such as Muslims in Britain.

LATIN AMERICA

Magical realism is most commonly associated with the geographical region of Latin America. It is a common misconception that all magical realism is Latin American and that it originated particularly in tropical regions of Central America. All the same, it must be acknowledged that Latin America is an important location for magical realist literary production. The Nobel Prize winning Gabriel García Márquez who has come to epitomize the image of magical realism, has influenced many writers to adopt the mode due to his innovative use of the technique, and has reinforced the connection between magical realism and Latin American literature.

Because Latin America has a form of postcolonial relationship with Europe, and particularly in relation to the colonial power of Spain from whence many of its inhabitants migrated, it has had, until the mid-twentieth century, a relationship with Europe that placed it on the margins of European perception, knowledge and culture. The shift away from a position of marginal cultural production in which all things European were esteemed, coincided with the development of magical realist fiction in Latin America. The emergence of an internationally recognized literary tradition in Latin America, known as the 'boom' of the 1950s and 1960s, was due to the interest in narrative and novelistic experimentation, including magical realism. The fiction of this period became known as the 'new novel' and is generally considered to be a modernist movement due to the attitude of the writers who sought to break away from previous literary traditions and to find a new means of expression. However, the style of their writing is often considered to be postmodern due to the narrative techniques they employed in which they play with the expectations of the reader, particularly in relation to time and the structure of the plots. As the critic Naomi Lindstrom explains in her book *Twentieth Century Spanish American Fiction*, 'Boom writing is *modern* in its ambitious drive to create major works of fiction whose innovative force would drive art forward into the future and secure a place in the history of narrative' (1994: 141). It is a matter of debate whether the literature became internationally acclaimed because of the widespread use of such experimentation or whether such techniques were employed in order to gain international recognition following the first successes of the 'boom'. Indeed, the roots of magical realism in Latin America go back before the boom of the 1960s to as early as the 1920s and the influence of Franz Roh's magic realism on a number of cosmopolitan writers. At a time when Latin American writing was developing in many countries as a distinct tradition from that of Spain, this mode of fiction became closely associated with the development of a Latin American literary tradition. So, although there are many individual national traditions in the Spanish-speaking Americas, it is appropriate here to discuss this writing as Latin American fiction due to the close connections between writers of its different countries and the writers' travels from country to country. For instance, Colombian García Márquez's ground-breaking novel *One Hundred Years of Solitude* was written in Mexico in 1967 and published in Argentina in 1970. Even before its publication, it was read and acclaimed by the Mexican writer Carlos Fuentes and Cuban Julio Cortazar. Later, in 1970, the Peruvian writer Mario Vargas Llosa wrote a book about García Márquez which acknowledged his position in Latin American literature (Williams 1985: 11).

Even in the early stages of magical realist writing in Latin America, the Cuban writer Alejo Carpentier created a distinction between European magic realist writing and Latin American magical realist writing that he defined and named *lo real maravilloso americano* which translates as 'American marvellous realism'. He saw European magic realism as 'tiresome pretension' unconnected in magical content to its cultural context of production (1995a: 89). Seeing Europe as a rational place where magic consisted of fairy-tale myths, he considered European magic realists to be creating a sense of mystery through narrative technique rather than cultural beliefs. In the years building up to the Cuban revolution in 1959, Carpentier, who was heavily involved in the artistic development of an expression of Latin American and Cuban independence, wrote his most famous magic realist novel *El reino de este mundo* (*The Kingdom of this World*) ([1949] 1975). In the prologue (reprinted in Zamora and Faris 1995) to this novel he made a statement that broke away from the influence of Roh's magic realism and established a new form of magical realism that was specific to and arose out of a Latin American context:

> Because of the virginity of the land, our upbringing, our ontology, the Faustian presence of the Indian and the black man, the revelation constituted by its recent discovery, its fecund racial mixing [*mestizaje*], America is far from using up its wealth of mythologies. After all, what is the entire history of America if not a chronicle of the marvellous real?
>
> (Carpentier 1995a: 88)

In this novel, set in Haiti during a historically recognized slave rebellion in the 1800s, he incorporates many elements of African American cultural and belief practices, particularly voodoo. Following elements of West African mythology which are present in African American folklore, Carpentier's characters are shape-shifters, changing shape at will, and are able to fly away when they die. The central figure, Ti Noel, although partially sceptical about voodoo, has been taught aspects of African mythology by his magically gifted mentor Mackandal in order to empower him during the slave revolt.

For Carpentier, this context of a mixture of cultures, the '*criollo*', or the '*mestizaje*', is what he considers to be at the heart of the spirit of Latin America that makes magical realism such an apt mode of fiction to express its culture. As he claims, the cross-cultural influences of the indigenous population, the Europeans and the African Caribbean and multi-racial peoples of the Latin Americas, and particularly his Caribbean region, lend an excess and exuberance of detail that he claims is 'baroque' in spirit:

> And why is Latin America the chosen territory of the baroque? Because all symbiosis, all *mestizaje*, engenders the baroque. The American baroque develops along with the *criollo* culture, with the meaning of *criollo*, with the self-awareness of the American man . . .; the awareness of being Other, of being new, of being symbiotic, of being a *criollo*.
>
> (Carpentier 1995b: 100)

Here he understands the baroque to be an artistic style that uses heavy and rich detail and ornamentation. Taking the highly ornate Mayan and Aztec sculptures of the god Quetzalcoatl as an example, he claims that they represent the complexities and large scale of the Mayan and Aztec culture and belief systems, and the scale, colours and variety of flora, fauna and landscape of the Americas. As he says, 'America, a continent of symbiosis, mutations, vibrations, *mestizaje* has always been baroque' (Carpentier 1995b: 98). The Latin American baroque style alluded to by Carpentier results from the indigenous people's architecture and visual art, and in particular its exuberance of detail and grandiose scale. In fact, he goes as far as to claim that the baroque and magical realism are 'essentially' present in Latin America. He states that the 'marvellous real is encountered in its raw state, latent and omnipresent, in all that is Latin American. Here the strange is commonplace, and always was commonplace' (Carpentier 1995b: 104).

This idea stems from a very colonial and European source, that of the letters of the 'conquistador' Hernando Cortés. In his letters to King Charles V of Spain on arriving in Latin America in 1519, Cortés claimed to be lacking the words to describe the new sights and experiences of the 'newly discovered' continent (Carpentier 1995b: 105). In a moment of colonial might, Cortés defined the Americas by stating that they were beyond the limits of European knowable experience. Influenced by Cortés and claiming that Latin America needs a new vocabulary, Carpentier reveals his own position as a European American, with an interest in and understanding of certain other American peoples, but ultimately from within a Euro-centric perspective (1995b: 105). This complicates his claim that European magic realists produce 'artificial' forms of magic realism, unconnected to their everyday reality, whereas Latin Americans write magical realism stemming from their context and experience. As the critic Amaryll Chanady points out, Carpentier himself constructs the naïve notion of an essentialist Latin American magical realism in order to distinguish Latin American cultural production from that of Europe. He does this with the purpose of claiming postcolonial cultural independence from Europe for Latin America. His contention is that Latin American baroque is a form of art that is vital and revolutionary because it breaks through borders by always expanding out from itself (Carpentier 1995b: 93). His position is a complicated balancing act between acknowledging and dismissing his influences in European culture, and desiring to create a stronger sense of an indigenous Latin American culture. This task is made all the more difficult as Latin American culture is in itself a mixture of influences from Iberian settlers, African slaves and native indigenous tribes such as the Mayans.

This balancing act was perhaps even harder for Guatemalan novelist Miguel Angel Asturias (1899–1974), whose magic realist writing is closely connected to the European post-expressionist form of Franz Roh and yet whose subject-matter attempts to incorporate Mayan mythology and the history of the colonial oppression of the indigenous people of Guatemala into Spanish language literature and the Latin American consciousness. His novel *Hombres de maiz* (*Men of Maize*) ([1949] 1988) is based upon the *Popol-Vuh* sacred almanac of the Mayans and adopts a plot structure typical of traditional indigenous storytelling. Rather than a linear plot structure that follows events chronologically from the same narrative perspective, this form of plot structure consists of seemingly unrelated stories that when brought together at the end or collated by the reader provide a complete story. His characters are surrounded by stimulation from Mayan mythology, whether they are open to it or not. Similar to Carpentier's Mandingue character Mackandal, Asturias' Gaspar Ilom is representative of an indigenous resistance to the colonial oppression and disenfranchisement of Native Latin Americans and is endowed with the magical powers of a shape-shifter. In *Men of Maize* the magical realist aspect arises from the cross-cultural context of the European perspective being influenced by and influencing that of the Mayan. For instance, there are several instances of runaway wives in the novel. A large section of the novel involves a husband's search for his lost wife after he has lost his land to colonialists. This plot structure reflects the Mayan myth of the 'rain woman' or 'mother of maize' who is lost to the worlds of the earth and the sky and lives caught between the two. It emphasizes the association of the man's loss of his wife with the loss of his land and ability to grow maize. The novel ends when the man seeking his wife finds 'rain woman'. In this instant the man appears to be reunited with the earth after having his land taken from him by colonialists. Because the effects of colonization and the story of rain woman from Mayan mythology are intertwined in this denouement, the depth of the effects of colonization on both the colonizers and the indigenous people is revealed in the novel. As Naomi Lindstrom notes, 'in *Men of Maize* the mythic outlook of the Indians is so powerfully stimulating to the imagination that even whites who consciously reject indigenous ways absorb some aspects of the Indians' vision' (1994: 101).

The interconnectedness of the literary terms of 'magical realism' and 'the new novel' has additionally created a debate in Latin American criticism concerning what constitutes magical realism. As Philip Swanson writes:

> If there is anything which defines the new novel in Latin America or unites its disparate manifestations, it is the desire somehow to re-evaluate or reject the values, belief systems and formal or stylistic patterns that lie at the roots of traditional realism.
>
> (1995: 3)

Frequently, such as in the criticism of Angel Flores first published in 1955, the term magical realism is used to refer to works by Argentinian Jorge Luis Borges. Borges' writing is acknowledged to be influential for magical realist writers and almost all Latin American writers in the late twentieth century, but it is much better described in specific terms of the new novel's experimentalism, and his own involvement with the avant-garde. Borges is best known for his meta-fictional narratives that challenge the reader's perception of what an author and a book are. For instance, in his selection of writings *A Universal History of Infamy* ([1935] 1975) he collects together stories ascribed to other authors whereas in fact he has created them himself. He claims that his writing is 'baroque' as it tries to 'exhaust all its possibilities' and is essentially intellectual (Borges 1975: 11). The stories include an extract verging on magical realism that recounts the creation of 'a map of the Empire that was of the same Scale as the Empire' and 'in the western Deserts, tattered Fragments of the Map are still to be found' (Borges 1975: 131). However, the fact that the reader knows that the extracts are deceptive as they are not by the author to which they are ascribed diminishes the realist element of the tales upon which the magical realism relies.

The writing of Gabriel García Márquez is seen to move towards a new direction for Latin American literature after the new novel despite his involvement in his younger days with the Latin American avant-garde. His most famous magical realist novel, *Cien años de soledad* (*One Hundred Years of Solitude*) ([1967] 1972), is considered to be the turning point of the 'new novel' away from fiction in which emphasis was placed on the experimental, and towards fiction that was politically and socially motivated, particularly dealing with folklore and the '*pueblo*' (common people) but yet which also included experimental techniques. The difference of style between the writing of Carpentier and García Márquez's magical realist writing reveals the full extent of the problem of assuming that Latin American magical realism can be discussed as one uncomplicated category. Carpentier's writing is predominantly realist with some magical happenings that are treated with awe such as a slave rebel flying away from his prospective killers witnessed by his amazed and delighted followers, whereas García Márquez's writing has an overwhelming atmosphere of nostalgia, and magical happenings such as the birth of a child with a tail occur as a matter of everyday reality. *One Hundred Years of Solitude* is a family history that begins with a typical mixture of the quaint and the horrific in a moment of nostalgia: 'Many years later, as he faced the firing squad, Colonel Aureliano Buendía was to remember that distant afternoon when his father took him to discover ice' (García Márquez 1972: 1). Moreover, coming out of the highly traumatized country of Colombia, and writing about long periods of civil unrest such as the War of A Thousand Days (1899–1902) and government brutality known as '*la violencia*' (1948–58), his magical realist exuberance is not only a celebration of the diversity of Latin America, as it is for Carpentier, but a way to express the excessive violence and confusion of Colombian, and Latin American, politics. During his Nobel Lecture 'The Solitude of Latin America' in 1982, García Márquez explained how the horrific past and present of much of Latin America lends itself to magical realism due to its ability to convey the 'unearthly tidings of Latin America' (1982b: 88).

Moreover, for García Márquez, magical realism was not a way to express the abundant mix of cultures that Carpentier saw in Cuba with his European Cuban perspective, but a way of expressing his own cultural context, using the oral storytelling techniques of his grandmother. García Márquez explains this, saying 'I realized that reality is also the myths of the common people, it is the beliefs, their legends; they are their every-day life and they affect their triumphs and failures' (in conversation with E. Gonzalez Bermejo, Williams 1985: 79). García Márquez grew up in his grandparents' huge and supposedly haunted house, in an atmosphere of superstition. The house was in the town of Aracataca in the coastal region of Colombia, which, as the critic Raymond L. Williams points out, is a perfect physical setting for magical realism: 'A synthesis of African and Hispanic cultures, with aspects of all centuries from the Middle Ages to the present, this region is viewed even by Colombians as a distinct and exotic part of the nation' (1985: 7).

The location of his childhood became the basis for García Márquez's fictional town of Macondo which recurs in several of his novels, and most particularly is the setting for *One Hundred Years of Solitude*. In this rural and tropical location, there are three sources for García Márquez's magical realism: a confusion of time scales that suggests a mythic time; a mixture of superstition, gossip and exaggeration; and the shock of the new. The first type of magical realism includes characters who live for years beyond the usual life-span. The second type includes occasions when characters fear their child will be born with a pig's tail as a result of incest, when an entire town becomes insomniac and is saved by a magic potion from the enigmatic gypsy Melquíades, and when it rains continuously for years on end. Here, rather than the mysterious marvellous realism of Carpentier, García Márquez tells all the stories in a matter-of-fact narratorial voice and includes exact detail to strengthen the claims. One of the many incidental matter-of-fact magical moments of the text includes the story of a priest who can levitate after drinking chocolate: 'he wiped his lips with a handkerchief that he drew from his sleeve, extended his arms, and closed his eyes. Thereupon Father Nicanor rose six inches above the level of the ground' (García Márquez 1972: 85). In fact, the only things which are considered extraordinary in this town provide the third source of magical realism: the scientific inventions brought to Macondo by Melquíades. The character José Arcadio Buendía is amazed by ice, and by a telescope, and is even considered to be mad by his wife Ursula when he tells her that the earth is round. Raymond L. Williams suggests that this third source of magical realism can be associated with the ideas of Franz Roh since the attitude portrayed is one in which the magic of everyday things is emphasized (1985: 77).

Although some critics accuse García Márquez of writing novels that lose their political power due to his nostalgia and whimsy of magical realism, others find the magical realism to be a powerful form of indirect political resistance. His writing often concerns historical tragedies such as civil wars, the rule of a dictator or an act of brutality by the army against its own people; for example, *One Hundred Years of Solitude* includes an account of a banana workers' strike in García Márquez's coastal region during the civil war when the army shot and killed many of the strikers. Due to denial by the military regime that the event took place, a lack of official records and the unreliability of speculation in the region, the exact number of workers killed is not known. In García Márquez's version although the massacre is witnessed by José Arcadio, he can later find no one to agree with what he saw and the massacre becomes a myth of little interest to the people. Here, García Márquez is playing with the idea of denial, taking it to an extreme where denial is transformed into complete ignorance. This can be seen as an example of the way in which magical realism can reflect the manipulation of reality by a corrupt government, with the willing connivance of the population until there can no longer be a believable version of events, only conflicting accounts or denials. García Márquez's novel *El otoño del patriarca* (*The Autumn of the Patriarch*) ([1975] 1978) is written with this form of corruption of reality and truth in mind. Following a tradition initiated by Miguel Angel Asturias, García Márquez, being deeply affected by the corruption and violence he witnessed through the rule of dictators, wrote an exaggerated baroque tale of the archetypal dictator who in the case of the novel lives for hundreds of years. His source material was close at hand in Latin America where García Márquez witnessed and was affected by several dictatorships: of Venezuelan Juan Vicente Gomez, the aftermath of the death of the Colombian dictator Perez Jimenez in 1958, the appalling treatment of the Chilean people by Colonel Pinochet in the 1970s, and by stories of the Liberal leader General Uribe Uribe who was admired by his grandfather. Stories of such dictators included the legends they and their followers propagated about themselves to mythologize the leader, the hushed-up horrors perpetrated in order to maintain their leadership, and the resulting antics of an all-powerful and paranoid man. *The Autumn of the Patriarch* is less magical realist than *One Hundred Years of Solitude* in that it contains fewer magical happenings. On the other hand, the manipulation of truth by the patriarch and the exuberance of detail create an exaggerated and exotic atmosphere where reality is unstable. For instance, it is actually unclear how many patriarchs there have been as the president appears to live an impossibly long time and yet he also has a body-double to make it appear that he is present everywhere in the land. The instability of reality caused by the manipulation of truth by politicians in this novel is not typical of magical realist writing. Rather, magical realist fiction relies upon the readers' trust and acceptance of the forms of fictional reality offered to them. When reality is seen to be manipulated in the text, as it is in *The Autumn of the Patriarch*, the reader will naturally doubt the veracity of magical happenings. This novel is also different from *One Hundred Years of Solitude* in that it diverges from the oral story-telling structure. There are no paragraph breaks in the text, which produces an overwhelmingly intense effect that is increased by the continuous use of detail and ever changing story-line.

General Uribe Uribe is also thought to be the inspiration for Colonel Aureliano Buendía of *One Hundred Years of Solitude*. As the critic Stephen Minta points out, both military heroes in fact lost all their wars and yet maintained an aura of glory (1987: 14). It is through the story of one of the main characters of the novel, Colonel Buendía, that the endless and pointless warring between political factions that has driven the violent history of Colombia is criticized by García Márquez. He reveals the differences between the two warring parties to be ridiculously slight, so much so that Aureliano Buendía cannot understand their differences. However, García Márquez also reveals the haphazard and fervent way in which people choose their political allegiances without regard for the political debates, which leads to disastrous and violent consequences. Aureliano's father-in-law tells him that 'The liberals, . . . were Free-masons, bad people, wanting to hang priests' whereas the Conservatives 'had received their power directly from God' (García Márquez 1972: 98). Aureliano chooses to become a liberal because he is told that they wanted to recognize illegitimate children. Ultimately, Aureliano dedicates his life to fighting for the Liberals, only in later life to realize 'He had had to start thirty-two wars and had had to violate all of his pacts with death and wallow like a hog in the dungheap of glory in order to discover the privileges of simplicity almost forty years late' (García Márquez 1972: 174).

In contrast, García Márquez incorporates folklore into *One Hundred Years of Solitude* rather than authorized beliefs from, for instance, organized religion. This allows for the voices of under- or un-represented people, such as the politically un-represented and culturally marginalized people of the Colombian Caribbean coast, to be expressed in the novel. Philip Swanson notes that García Márquez's magical realism:

> must be a political question of reinterpretation of reality, utilizing the oral style inherited from his grandmother's fantastic story-telling, García Márquez seems to want to reproduce a traditional, popular rural perspective – challenging the hegemony of the alien, dominant, imported culture and reinstating the value of the community's own cultural perspective.
>
> (1995: 12)

In his later novel, *Crónica de una muerte anunciada* (*Chronicle of a Death Foretold*) ([1981] 1982a), García Márquez breaks away from politics altogether, concentrating rather on an account of how a town in the coastal region of Colombia failed to stop the death of a young lover because of a traditional and archaic sense of 'honour', inertia or hypocrisy. This book represents a departure from the previous style and content of García Márquez's fiction, as it is written in a linear narrative, with fewer magical events or assumptions. However, it retains a sense of connection to the coastal region and the people's tenacious adherence to centuries-old Spanish notions of chivalry and honour.

The first woman writer from Latin America to be recognized outside the continent, Isabel Allende, is also known as a magical realist. Her most notable magical realist novel *La casa de los espíritus* (*The House of the Spirits*) ([1982] 1986) is a popularization of García Márquez's style of magical realism, where unlike García Márquez, the emphasis is placed on the accessibility of the plot and emotional effect of the novel. Written a few years after *Chronicle of a Death Foretold*, *The House of the Spirits* is considered to be a part of the 'post-boom' of Latin American fiction. Following the 'boom' of popularity of the modernist experimental 'high-brow' 'new novel', the fiction of the 'post-boom' is often associated with postmodern self-reflexive playful narratives and the introduction of the popular into fiction. *The House of the Spirits* is not written in a post-modern style but owes much to the style of García Márquez in relation to the attention to detail and occasional nostalgia. Allende herself is a member of the Chilean ruling classes and as the goddaughter and cousin of ex-President Salvador Allende, her novel takes up the perspective of the disenfranchised of Chile during the time of dictatorship and civil unrest. The novel was written during the time of police brutality, and of the murders of some of those who opposed the government of Colonel Pinochet. It follows the stories of three generations of women and their peasant or working-class lovers, ending in the time of a modern-day dictatorship. Many of the male figures, and eventually, the final generation of female characters, are political revolutionaries, first as a peasant class resisting the abuse of a cruel landlord, and finally as left-wing revolutionaries fighting against the brutality and corruption of the right-wing dictatorship. Since Allende experienced at first-hand the effects of a military coup on her personal and family life when her relative President Salvador Allende was ousted in a coup in 1973, and she has since lived in exile, it is not surprising that her novels tell the story of the effects of political unrest on the women of Chile.

Similarities between *The House of the Spirits* and *One Hundred Years of Solitude* are often noted by critics. There is the repetition of names from one generation to the next, and the structure of the novel around a family saga. However, Philip Swanson also points out that Allende appears to be rejecting García Márquez's influence by placing more emphasis on a popular and less literary style, and by bringing into question the magical realist elements of her novel (1995: 161). The novel opens with the magical realist setting in which ghosts, extraordinary happenings and extrasensory perception are commonplace. The majority of the novel has a similar nostalgic narrative style to *One Hundred Years of Solitude* including much superstition, exaggeration and excessive detail. The arrival of the character Clara's enormous dog is described as a truly extraordinary event but it is also linked to a very domestic scene: 'Some people believed him to be a cross between a dog and a mare, and expected him to sprout wings and horns and acquire the sulfuric breath of a dragon, like the beasts Rosa was embroidering on her endless tablecloth' (Allende 1986: 33). The title of *The House of the Spirits* refers to the spiritual world of a clairvoyant and communicator with the dead, Clara, who reappears in the family house as a ghost to influence the next generation. It is only during the time of the third generation of women, and Clara's granddaughter Alba, who is a revolutionary against the right-wing dictator, that the atmosphere of the novel changes. In this section of the novel, the full horror of the brutality of the government against its people is communicated in a realist narrative. In this section, reality and truth are so manipulated by the government that Allende leaves behind the magical realism of the spiritual world in favour of emphasizing the effects of military rule and propaganda on people's perception of reality. While recording the events of imprisonment in a women's jail the narrator considers the effects of living with brutality has upon children. In the jail she tells 'magic stories' to the children of an insane inmate and considers: 'the fate of the children growing up in that place with a mother who has gone mad' (Allende 1986: 484). By doing so, Allende avoids using García Márquez's nostalgic magical realist style during the passages of her book where she portrays state brutality. But even in the prison Alba is keen to maintain a link with the magical stories of her ancestors and does so by passing them on to her inmate's children. Swanson also reminds us that Alba is keen to interpret her grandmother's diaries and incorporate her spiritual power and the magical realism for a practical purpose:

> Clara's spiritualism, on one level, simply represents happy times which are destroyed by natural and political cataclysms. The world of the spirits, in other words, is the sort of ideal place the world should be. In the meantime, the positive force of Clara's spiritualism needs to be harnessed on a practical and political level.
>
> (1995: 163)

The main narrative of the novel is a means by which the narrator, Alba, relates her grandmother's diaries, telling how she came into possession of them. The narrative, which thus consists of a series of magical tales, represents a use of the diaries themselves as a vehicle for political comment.

Another novel which begins with the handing-down of a book by a female to the succeeding generations of her family, and the subsequent use of the material to tell a family saga, is Laura Esquivel's *Como agua para chocolate* (*Like Water for Chocolate*) ([1989] 1993). Esquivel's novel is written from a women's perspective with a female narrator and concerning the domestic lives of women. Therefore, like Allende's, it is very much a novel about the under-represented. Written in Mexico, it is a post-boom novel in that it incorporates into the narrative recipes as monthly instalments from popular women's magazines at the beginning of each chapter. The narrative, in fact, proceeds from the recipe instructions and relates the tragic love affair of the character Tita, the cook and recipe writer, and her sister's husband. Tita, who is not permitted to marry her lover because her mother wishes her to stay at home and look after her, has to witness her sister marry him instead. Her unrequited love and ostracism from the family lead her to harness her extraordinary powers, which are described using the magical realist matter-of-fact narrative style. Esquivel employs the magical realist tactic of Salman Rushdie, to extend metaphors into a real state, although her prose is less exuberant and contains less incidental detail than Rushdie's. For instance, Tita's food communicates her emotions to such an extent that the people who eat it enact her emotions for her. After eating the wedding cake which Tita made while suffering from unrequited love, the wedding guests all suffer from 'a wave of longing': 'the weeping was just the first symptom of a strange intoxication – an acute attack of pain and frustration – that seized the guests and scattered them across the patio' (Esquivel 1993: 39). Like the writing of the Chicano Spanish-speaking people on the other side of the United States/Mexico border, Esquivel also includes Native Mexican/American characters who provide alternative medicines and magic to help those in need. The rejected and deceased grandmother of Tita's fiancé John is a Native woman who sits with Tita as she recovers from a mental breakdown. This is the grandmother who shares her secret recipe for matches to create the passion that John shares with Tita. Thus the novel tells the stories of the domestic lives of women living on the margins of their families and society, whether they are rejected by their racist and socially ambitious families, as in the case of John's grandmother, or because of patriarchal constraints, as in the case of Tita. Although this story takes place in one household of women, the political world intrudes and they are often visited by soldiers from both sides of the war demanding food and shelter. This story is set in an undefined period of time against the backdrop of a seemingly interminable civil war which threatens their safety. Even here, in this most domestic setting, the politics of Latin America makes its mark in a magical realist novel.

THE ENGLISH-SPEAKING WORLD

Magical realism in literature in the English language appeared first in the early 1970s in Canada, West Africa and the United States and now spans many locations across the globe. Notable locations of magical realism are Canada, the Caribbean, West Africa, South Africa, India, the United States and England, with acknowledged magical realist writing also being produced in Australia and New Zealand. Unlike Latin American magical realism, there has not been a long enough tradition in the English language to make it possible to trace influences from one English-language magical realist to another. Probably the best-known writer of magical realism in the English language is the British-Indian writer Salman Rushdie. As a writer who accepts the term's application to his writing, he is also clear about his influences in relation to this mode: Nobel Prize winners Gabriel García Márquez, the German novelist and playwright Günter Grass, and the Russian novelist Mikhail Bulgakov (1891–1940). It is apparent from the history of magical realism outlined earlier that Rushdie's English language form of magical realism straddles both the surrealist tradition of magic realism as it developed in Europe and the mythic tradition of magical realism as it developed in Latin America. This is typical of magical realist writing in English since because it appears later than its counterparts in Europe and Latin America, it frequently produces forms of magical realism that combine influences from writers across the globe.

However, what unites these writers is the political nature of the magical realism that is written in these locations, whether from an overtly anti-imperial, feminist or Marxist approach, or a mixture of all of these, or whether the form reveals its political aspect more covertly through the cultural politics of postcolonialism, cross-culturalism, or the friction between the writing of pragmatic European Western culture and oral, mythic based cultures. What locates these writers politically is their narrative position outside the dominant power structures and cultural centres. This includes the case of Salman Rushdie, who, although he is located at the centre of cultural production, his narrators and subject matter are located outside it. It also includes Angela Carter (1940–92), the most celebrated English feminist writer of the 1980s and 1990s, who wrote carnivalesque, exuberant magical realist narratives influenced by the comedies of William Shakespeare and the literary theories of the Russian Mikhail Bakhtin. In *Nights at the Circus* ([1984] 1994) the story follows the life of a working-class girl who develops real wings and becomes a trapeze artist in a circus. In the novel *Wise Children* ([1991] 1992) the story is told from the working-class feminist perspective of an septogenarian woman who has cataclysmic house-destroying sex with her even older 'aristocratic' uncle. Both of these novels are set in the mid-twentieth century in Britain at the end of the British Empire when imperialist ideas of the assumed superiority of British patriarchy still exerted a strong influence over society. The next chapter of this book will consider in more detail how the magical realism of Carter's narratives, in combination with the carnivalesque and the literary theories of Bakhtin provides her with a weapon with which to attack and overturn accepted gender and social roles, and particularly those associated with imperialism.

What often connects English language magical realists with each other is their opposition to British colonialism in countries such as India, Canada, Australia and the regions of West Africa and the Caribbean. This prevalence of magical realist writing in English in postcolonial nations has given rise to a debate concerning the suitability of magical realism as a postcolonial strategy of writing. This debate and its relation to the development of magical realist writing will be explored in more detail in the following chapters. In addition, writers currently in conditions of oppression in the United States, such as Native American, Chicano and African Americans, have also adopted magical realism as a means to write against dominant American culture. Because of this, there are many similarities between anti-British-colonial magical realist writing, and anti-neo-American-colonial magical realist writing, since both groups of writers are concerned with the incorporation of oral culture and indigenous myth into the dominant Western cultural form of the novel.

The majority of magical realist writing cannot be said to occupy the mainstream of these countries' literary production. In Indian writing, for instance, Salman Rushdie, Amitav Ghosh and Arundhati Roy are very notable prize winning writers and all are writers of magical realism, but they do not constitute a movement or group in Indian literature, each being unconnected to the other and located in different countries. Rushdie lives between England, India and New York. Ghosh lives between the United States and India, and Roy remains in India. Thus, Rushdie and Ghosh tend to be considered as diasporic Indian writers whose writing is influenced by their hybrid cultural context. In fact, the transnational and transcultural lives of many of the English language magical realist writers make it difficult to situate them in any one country's literary tradition.

The exception to the rule is the situation of magical realism in Canadian literature, where it has become recognized as a 'sub-genre' of Canadian Literature (Andrews 1999: 1). In the 1970s, at a time when Canadian writers were attempting to conceive of a sense of Canadian nationhood divorced from British colonialism, Robert Kroetsch and Jack Hodgins in the Canadian west, away from the centre of power in the eastern cities of Toronto, Ottawa and Quebec, were writing magical realist fiction. Kroetsch and Hodgins introduced an unashamedly postmodern postcolonial form of magical realism. Kroetsch's use of the magical realist mode in his novel *What the Crow Said* (1978) was a deliberate choice, following the influence of García Márquez, specifically to find a mode of fiction that would provide a means to express both the marginal perspective of rural western Canadians, and also the Canadian perspective in relation to Britain and to the powerful neo-colonial neighbour, the United States. Kroetsch is very explicit about the influence of García Márquez and about the deliberate choice to employ his style of magical realism as a narrative strategy. Kroetsch's criticism, poetry and fiction all ask questions about how to write about, and in, a country that is new and uncertain of its national identity. Coming from a settler and, in his case German community, he senses the hostility of the environment, a lack of historical connection to it but paradoxically a reliance upon it. Considering these problems, he asks questions such as 'What might be the narrative strategies that locate the Canadian experience and psyche and language in a body of writing?' (Kroetsch

1989: 179). In his notes on writing the novel, *Crow Journals*, he claims that García Márquez had solved the problem of how to write in the third person without seeming to impose a 'strict sense of point of view' and García Márquez's narrative mode had provided the means to 'forget the conventions of realism' (1980: 3 May 1974). This enabled Kroetsch to write from a marginal perspective without having to battle against the values and cultural assumptions of the colonial influence of Britain. The critic Jeanne Delbaere notes that there are traceable similarities between *What the Crow Said* and García Márquez's *One Hundred Years of Solitude*. She points to the first sentence of *What the Crow Said* to illustrate the influence of García Márquez, noting particularly the reliance of the narrator on a past and seemingly unconnected event for the causality of the whole of the story to follow: 'People, years later, blamed everything on the bees; it was the bees, they said, seducing Vera Lang, that started everything' (Kroetsch 1978: 1). This refers to the typically magical happening of the impregnation of a girl called Vera by bees in the town of Big Indian. The novel itself traces the collective memory of the town of Big Indian over a period of twenty-five years and includes impossibly long card-games, extremely high floods, tower building, and eccentric characters' tales all told through a matter-of-fact narrative. Although, following García Márquez's narrative mode, Kroetsch writes a very specifically 'Canadian' novel. This Canadian magical realism is set 'ambiguously on the border' between two provinces in an indeterminate zone, in a climate and landscape that is in itself extreme in its harshness and flatness. Here, the 'tall tale' is the narrative form that predominates in local settler oral culture and this is exactly what Kroetsch employs to create a magical realism of the Canadian west. His characters relay stories of extraordinary events in the down-to-earth settings of the locality. Often these events are acts of nature such as a tornado or a plague of salamanders. Although these events are explicable, they are narrated as though they are extraordinary. As Delbaere comments, the extreme flatness of the landscape and hardship of their lives makes the men of the township strive 'to defeat the horizontality of their everyday life by drinking, playing cards, telling stories and trying to escape upwards' (1992: 93).

Jack Hodgins' adoption of magical realism in his novel *The Invention of the World* ([1977] 1986) is overtly anti-colonialist. It follows the story of a community called 'The Revelations Colony of Truth' run by a tyrannical figure who, although seemingly a magical saviour figure for people from Ireland looking for a better life in the 'New World', repeats the history of colonization by virtually enslaving the people who live in his community. This novel, like Kroetsch's, is set in a small community on the edges of wilderness. In fact, from the very beginning of the novel, Hodgins explains that the population's connection with the wilderness has led them to lose contact with the realities of urban and community life, going 'bush crazy'. Hodgins, who was also influenced by Latin American magical realism, begins his novel with a similar enigmatic statement to that of *One Hundred Years of Solitude.* He begins by stating 'Donal Keneally's mother started it all, a hundred and fifty years ago and thousands of miles away' (Hodgins 1986: x). The magical realism in the novel is found in relation to the myths that are told about the leader of the Colony, Keneally. On finding Keneally as a new-born baby, sitting up and 'condemning the world' with his fierce stare, an old woman considers 'This is impossible . . . but as her whole lifetime had been a series of impossibilities from the beginning she merely stopped to pick him up' (Hodgins 1986: 72). Although no one knows either the woman involved, who is later killed by him, or his mother who goes missing after his birth, his conception by a satanic-looking bull and his strangely mature behaviour even immediately after his birth are known myths. The question relating to Keneally in the text is whether he is truly magical or whether he has created such myths around himself. The question remains unanswered. Even at the end of the novel, the central characters Maggie and Wade are led away from their wedding party by a man fitting the description of the dead Keneally, his identity is not confirmed and his magic remains an enigma. The novel, from the very beginning, brings into question the notion of truth, particularly in relation to the past. The narrator, Becker, attempts to piece together the recent past of his community through collecting all the stories, newspaper articles and radio transmissions that he can. He is aware, and makes the reader aware, that there are many versions of the past and that not all that is said can be proven, but that a personal version of the past can be found; 'He will absorb all this chaos, he will confront it and absorb it, and eventually he will begin to tell, and by telling release it, make it finally his own' (Hodgins 1986: x).

Magic realist cultural production already existed in Canada at the time of *What the Crow Said* and *The Invention of the World*, primarily as painting in the style of the German art critic Franz Roh's magic realism. This will be discussed in detail in Chapter 5. Since Kroetsch and Hodgins, magical realism has also recurred as a sub-genre in Canadian writing employed by writers with some position of marginality. Gail Anderson-Dargatz's novel *The Cure for Death by Lightning* ([1996] 1998) written in British Columbia, and Ann-Marie MacDonald's *Fall on Your Knees* (1996) written in the eastern Maritime provinces, both consider the position of women, and particularly lesbian women, in the poverty-struck and forgotten regions of Canada through their magical realist narratives.

Canadian magical realism shares with Britain, other postcolonial nations and the United States, a type of magical realism that has resulted from the cross-culturalism of these countries. In Canada, as in the United States, where the dominant culture is based upon an Anglo-European tradition, writers wishing to express one or more cultural influences which do not coincide with dominant pragmatic thinking often employ magical realism. As Canada is one of the most consciously multicultural nations in the world, and a nation marginalized by previous British colonialism and current American neo-colonialism, magical realism becomes a useful narrative device for expressing views that oppose the dominant ways of thinking. There is space even for contradiction in a magical realist text and so it allows for the expression of multiple cultural perspectives. For instance, Gail Anderson-Dargatz creates a magical realist narrative by incorporating local Native Canadian (known as First Nations) mythology into her characters' lives in *The Cure for Death by Lightning*. The non-First Nations narrator is terrified by violent happenings in the woods and accepts the local First Nations' explanation that it is the work of the mythical figure of Coyote, the shape-shifter who can change his appearance at will. This is not a celebration of magic but a novel describing the terror of women at the mercy of a malign magic that they believe exists.

Canadian cross-cultural magical realist writing is not always sinister; the most notable contemporary writer to be associated with magical realism in Canada, Michael Ondaatje, takes a celebratory view of the exuberance and exaggeration of the magic in oral storytelling. His writing often veers away from the definitions of magical realism presented in this book. Yet, although the events of the novel are infrequently magical or extraordinary, his writing consistently throws doubt on, and plays with, the notion of realism and truth, questioning the veracity of the family stories that he tells. In fact, there are examples in his family biography *Running in the Family* (1982) that are reminiscent of Latin American magical realism. For instance, the life of the narrator's grandmother is told with emphasis on her magical capabilities and excessiveness. The narrator's grandmother is introduced to the reader as a 'magical' person who 'could read thunder'. Having lived a life of excess she seeks a dramatic death and her body is found after a flood 'in the blue arms of a jacaranda tree' (Ondaatje 1982: 113). Building on the myth of a larger-than-life personality, Ondaatje comments that '[e]ven in her death her generosity exceeded the physically possible for she had donated her body to six hospitals' (1982: 123).

Where Ondaatje's work is recognizably magical realist, it is a form of magical realism that, in its exuberant and colourful content and setting, has more connection to Indian or Latin American magical realism than to that of the harsh Canadian west. Ondaatje, moreover, is associated with his transcultural background rather than his Canadian nationality: he was born into a mixed race Sri Lankan family and emigrated to Canada. The settings of his novels reflect this cosmopolitanism: Sri Lanka, the United States, Canada, war-torn Europe and North Africa, although his magical realist events are only set in Sri Lanka. The situation is similar for Salman Rushdie and his equally cosmopolitan compatriot Amitav Ghosh. Rushdie's writing is considered both British and Indian, as Ghosh's is considered both American and Indian. But, unlike Ondaatje's magical realism, the magical realist happenings in Rushdie and Ghosh's fiction occur in India, Pakistan, Britain and America.

The critic Kum Kum Sangari notes that, because of its inherent mixture of opposing perspectives, magical realist writing is the perfect form of writing for a cosmopolitan postcolonial middle-class emigrant writer such as Rushdie whose life has been influenced by British colonialism and Indian popular culture with all their multiplicities and contradictions (1987: 177). Rushdie himself is a highly political writer who is deeply concerned with the future of India and is fascinated by the diversity of its population, religions and languages. He explains that, '"My" India has always been based on ideas of multiplicity, pluralism,

hybridity' (Rushdie 1991: 32). *Midnight's Children* ([1981] 1982) provides the best illustration of a novel that attempts to provide a kind of
modern epic for a country that in the space of fifty years moved from a
new confident nation full of the promise of its diverse gifts to a nation
conscious of its own failings and on the verge of breaking down into a
multiplicity of conflicting factions. Rushdie's character Saleem, who is
born in 1947 as the nation of India comes into being, is part of a circle of
children born at the same time with magical gifts, not least the ability
of telepathy. Saleem is the narrator of the book, telling his and India's
tale retrospectively while working in a pickling factory. From the very
beginning of his life, Saleem witnesses and participates in many magical
things: his mother is told Saleem's future by a soothsayer before he is
born; he sees bodies disappearing; and he rides through the air with
a witch. Many of these features have their origin in magical tales such as
A Thousand and One Nights, but they are also associated with Indian
circus acts like the 'Indian rope trick'. His most characteristic form of
magical realism is what Marguerite Alexander calls his 'magic realization
of metaphor' in which Rushdie interprets a metaphor literally that is then
enacted in the narrative (1994: 5). His novel *The Satanic Verses* ([1988]
1992) relies heavily upon this narrative device. For instance Saladin
Chamcha is 'demonized' as an illegal immigrant and therefore evolves into
a devil-like goat when he is arrested by the British police. In a typically
magical realist narrative the police accept his devilish appearance as an
ordinary occurrence: 'What puzzled Chamcha was that a circumstance
which struck him as utterly bewildering and unprecedented – that is, his
metamorphosis into this supernatural imp – was being treated by the
others as if it were the most banal and familiar matter they could imagine'
(Rushdie 1992: 158).

Rushdie's work is well known for drawing on many European literary
and cultural influences which range from Laurence Sterne's *Tristram
Shandy* ([1769] 1983), Mikhail Bulgakov's *The Master and Margarita*
([1967] 1984), Günter Grass's *The Tin Drum* ([1959] 1965), as well as
García Márquez's *One Hundred Years of Solitude*. In addition, Rushdie
draws on Indian mythological epics such as *The Mahabharata* and even
Bollywood movies and Indian street life. In his study of Rushdie's work
the critic Timothy Brennan notes that Rushdie's novel *Shame* ([1983]
1984), set in Pakistan under a military dictatorship, is most notably

influenced by *One Hundred Years of Solitude*. He identifies at least nine similarities of plot between the two novels including the haunting of killers by those unjustly killed and the stories of popular generals and leaders who are shot through the chest but who do not die (Brennan 1989: 66). His writing, which is always set in an identifiable although often altered place such as 'Elloween Delloween' (London), mixes Western and Indian cultural perspectives, realism with mythology, high with low culture, written and oral, and real people with entirely fictional people. What this produces is a magical text in which the contradictions of contemporary India and Indianness are explored. As Sangari notes, in connection with *Midnight's Children*, 'the narrative embraces all mythologies in an effort to activate an essentially plural or secular conception of Indianness' (1987: 180).

Rushdie's status as an immigrant to Britain but writing about the Indian sub-continent allows him to position himself as both an 'insider' and an 'outsider' of both cultures. This hybrid identity allows him to take advantage of magical realism as the most appropriate style for his novels. Amitav Ghosh shares a similar insider/outsider position although his form of magical realism is less exuberant, and less ubiquitous than that of Rushdie. There are two sources of magical realism in Ghosh's *The Calcutta Chromosome* ([1995] 1997). The first source verges on science fiction, as Ghosh's novel includes extremely advanced computer technology which allows the computer to have its own personality and the ability to seek out globally the smallest fact in seconds. The second source is more mystical, and follows the story of a religious sect who are endowed with the capacity for metempsychosis in that they are able to transfer their souls from one body to another across generations. The narrative itself traces the story of a female Indian scientist who discovers the cause of malaria, but her English colonial employer takes the credit for this discovery.

Despite the appropriateness of magical realism as a narrative form for the cosmopolitan Indian writer, the specifically Indian writer Arundhati Roy has also adopted the form. Whilst also belonging to the Indian middle-class and being influenced by the writing of Salman Rushdie, Roy, who is from the south of India and who is not from the metropolis of Bombay or an immigrant to Britain, has remained predominantly in India and has written about her home state of Kerala. Her novel, the *The God of Small Things* (1997) concerns the trauma of childhood when caught in the strictures of the caste system and as such it, like Rushdie's, has a political dimension relating to life in the margins – in this case the position of two lovers meeting outside the control of the caste system with tragic results. The magical realist moments in her novel are in fact fewer than in Rushdie's work and Roy does not employ the magic realization of metaphor. Her narrative, however, allows the expansive and exuberant imagination of the child to be the measure of reality and thus includes a dead child cart-wheeling through a church. Roy's work is, as her title suggests, concerned with the local and the things considered insignificant in larger society, which reinforces its concern for the mistreatment of those in the margins of Indian society. As the magical realist narrative is told from the perspective of a naïve child it provides a critical commentary on and contrasts with the ugly world of Indian social prejudice.

On the African continent magical realism and postcolonialism have gone hand-in-hand particularly in West and South Africa. In West Africa, the Yoruba mythologies and beliefs in particular have provided material for other African writers such as Ben Okri and Amos Tutuola (1920–97). In addition to drawing on the western novel form and upon themes such as colonialism, religion and internationalism, West African magical realism often incorporates local influences to produce a cross-cultural literature that emulates the situation of many West Africans today. As the critic Brenda Cooper notes: 'African writers very often adhere to this animism, incorporate spirits, ancestors and talking animals, in stories, both adapted folktales and newly invented yarns, in order to express their passions, their aesthetics and their politics' (1998: 40). She claims that these stories are still prevalent due to the superficial influence on the local culture of colonialism in West Africa (Cooper 1998: 40). Because of this, although Okri is a British Nigerian who has lived in London for most of his life, his novel *The Famished Road* ([1991] 1992) is told predominantly from a West African perspective. The novel follows the struggles of an *abiku* child (a child attached both to the spirit world and the living world, who is born again only to die and return again) and the child's attempt to negotiate between the two forces from the living and the dead that seek to dominate him. The traditional West African mythological content and narrative perspective of the narrative lead some critics to question whether this is indeed a magical realist novel. The question of whether the mythological aspect is considered to be real or magical depends strongly on the cultural perspective of the reader. If the reader lives within a cultural context where magical happenings of the type portrayed in the novel are considered to be a possible aspect of reality and not magical at all, then the reader may not recognize the magical realist element of the narrative. I will return to this question in the final chapters of this book.

Because South Africa, unlike West African countries, has a significant history of European settlement, its colonial history and culture is notably different and as a consequence so too is its magical realist writing. Additionally, the need to reconsider its history and its mythologies in the light of the nation's new post-apartheid political conditions provides a motivation for Afrikaner writers to employ magical realist techniques. Magical realism is becoming more widely recognized in both English language and Afrikaans literature due to the English language publications of André Brink. Brink's novels *Imaginings in Sand* ([1996] 2000a) and *Devil's Valley* ([1999] 2000b) are attempts to rethink the position of Afrikaners in the new cross-cultural South Africa, particularly in relation to the denial of influence of indigenous African myth in a mainly strict protestant Christian context. Brink claims that South Africans have to reinvent the real and reconsider the past from an alternative perspective when trying to imagine a new South Africa. As the South African critic Marita Wenzel notes, Brink includes dead characters and ghosts amongst the living in his fictional Afrikaner communities in order to emphasize the relevance of the past to the present, in order to ensure that Afrikaners do not dismiss their role in the formation of both the old and the new South Africa (2002: 5).

The predominant and increasingly frequent form of magical realism in the United States tends to be written by cross-cultural women with a political agenda relating to gender and the marginalization of cultures. Due to the dominantly Anglo-European culture of the United States and its predominantly immigrant society, there are many cross-cultural groups which, like the African Americans, sense that they are marginalized and under- or misrepresented in Anglo-European American life. This is doubly true for cross-cultural women who face prejudice both as a member of a marginalized culture and as women. Although many reject the term now, there was an acceptance of the term 'magical realism' by many cross-cultural women writers in the United States during the late 1980s. Among these writers and their work, the Nobel Prize winner Toni Morrison writes magical realist narratives that draw from her cross-cultural context as an African American. Her narratives are influenced by African American oral culture and mythology adapted from West African culture. Morrison's *Song of Solomon* ([1977] 1989), *Beloved* ([1987] 1988) and *Jazz* ([1992] 1993) all have magical realist elements including the arrival of an *abiku* child, the presence of ghostly figures from the past, women with magical powers born without navels and men that can fly. These magical happenings are incorporated into books that have complex plot structures having also been influenced by a Western postmodernist style, and early twentieth-century canonical writers such as the southerner William Faulkner and the African American Ralph Ellison. This magical realism is employed by Morrison in order to create a specifically cross-cultural African American cultural memory with which to rebuild a sense of an African American community at a time of crisis, when the majority of the African American population seem to her to be held in a position of economic and spiritual poverty.

Magical realism is employed by these women writers to reflect the complex and sometimes paradoxical multiple cultural influences that they experience as cross-cultural American women. Finding herself trapped between the racist Anglo-European American and male dominated Chinese American cultures, Maxine Hong Kingston uses magical realism in her novel *The Woman Warrior: A Memoir of a Girlhood Among Ghosts* ([1976] 1981a) in order express the misrepresented history of Chinese America from an insider position in a community where discussion of the past is taboo. The narrator incorporates and adapts Chinese oral storytelling traditions, with many tales of ghosts, to her own Californian context with a view to creating a Chinese American communal memory. For instance, her mother tells her tales about ghosts that she encountered in China and imbues the tales with moral guidance for her daughter's American life. This mixture of Chinese, dominant American and the cross-cultural Chinese American child's perspectives, and the narrator's confusion regarding what is real and what is make-believe, creates a magical realist dimension to the text.

A third cross-cultural female writer who is often connected with Morrison and Hong Kingston is the mixed blood Native American writer

Leslie Marmon Silko. Silko's main magical realist text is her epic post-modern novel *The Almanac of the Dead* ([1991] 1992). Whilst proposing an environmental and community-building political viewpoint, this novel incorporates Native American, Native Mexican and even West African mythology and belief systems into the equally Anglo-European American text. The novel includes the story of a political movement to save the Mother Earth from misuse and ultimately from destruction by the Anglo-European Americans. The cultural and political perspective of the novel is in accord with the Native American belief in the spiritual intercon-nectedness and equality of all physical aspects of the environment and the animals that inhabit it. This is contrasted with the dominant cultural attitudes in America that treat the earth as a commodity and resource. The novel's magical realist plot follows the work of an 'eco-warrior' Native Mexican, Tacho, who gains his political power and guidance from reading the signs from his prayer bundles and listening to sacred macaw birds.

Such cross-cultural magical realist literature of the United States is closely related to that of Latin America, and particularly to that from countries in the region where the predominantly English-speaking and Spanish-speaking American continents join. The border region of the United States and Mexico has one of the largest cross-cultural and multi-lingual populations of the United States. Amongst this population are the Chicano people who are a Spanish speaking culturally mixed group subject to Mexican and Native American influences. Here, the influence of Latin American magical realism is strong, and can be found in the works of Chicano writers such as Ana Castillo, who lives in an area of the United States which was previously a part of Mexico. Castillo's *So Far From God* ([1993] 1994), set in a small Chicano town, includes aspects of Native American mythology such as the ability to change shape and take on the form of other animals at will known as shape-shifting, as well as the exuberance of characters with seemingly magical powers who bring themselves back from the dead: a plot device which is common in Latin American magical realism. In fact, Ana Castillo's work is more remi-niscent in setting and atmosphere of the work of Mexican novelist Laura Esquivel than other English language magical realist writers of the border region like Leslie Marmon Silko.

The same geographical proximity opens the possibility of a strong influence from the Spanish-speaking Caribbean and the Latin American

Caribbean as well as the English-speaking Caribbean. Both Pauline Melville and Wilson Harris, who are from different generations, provide very differing examples of the influence of magical realism in this region, although, again, both write from a cross-cultural background and are now based in Britain. The younger of them, Pauline Melville, has written three very different fictional works using the same magical realist techniques. Her first novel *The Ventriloquist's Tale* ([1997] 1998) is based in the same geographical terrain of the Caribbean coast as García Márquez, this time in Guyana, where she was born, rather than Colombia, and has the same exuberant narrative and richness of detail. The novel emphasizes the cross-cultural and multi-lingual aspects of Guyana and the influence of the Amerindian people on the beliefs of the country. The introductory 'Prologue' is written in a style imitating oral storytelling and provides an introduction to the narrator's carnivalesque excessive character, who even before his own birth was endowed with extraordinary gifts that allowed him to give guidance to his mother. Her collections of short stories *Shape-Shifter: Stories* (1990) and *The Migration of Ghosts* ([1998] 1999) are more international in their settings, including geographical locations such as London and Spain, but all the same they incorporate magical happenings narrated in a matter-of-fact style. Although Wilson Harris, another Guyanese who emigrated to Britain in 1959, receives more critical attention, particularly within postcolonial criticism, his magical realism is more closely associated with the surrealist form of marvellous realism of Alejo Carpentier. Harris' work such as *Jonestown* (1996) and the *Palace of the Peacock* ([1960] 1998), which draws on Amerindian mythology and Guyanese history, is known for its poetical, obscure and mystical qualities which mark its difference from the matter-of-fact narratives of other English-language magical realists such as Rushdie or Morrison.

Not all magical realists are notably cross-cultural. Some writers labelled 'magical realist' due to their portrayal of extraordinary happenings through a matter-of-fact narrative include the United States novelist of the 1960s, Richard Brautigan (1935–84). His fiction contains a bitter critique of American capitalism and idealism and revises American mythology through magical realist satire. His *Trout Fishing in America* ([1967] 1989) includes a passage in which he criticizes the appropriation of natural resources for economic gain by presenting the sale of a stream that is kept – in segments that include all the fish and mosquitoes – in a hardware store. Later, John Irving's *The World According to Garp* ([1978] 1999) celebrates excess, the 'baroque' and the incredible; all of which are characteristics linked with Latin American magical realism. These writers chose this narrative technique for literary effect without drawing on the belief systems or mythology of their cultural context. In this way, they can be associated with the European magic realists who adopted the technique as literary experimentalism.

MAINLAND EUROPE

On mainland Europe literary magic(al) realism is closely associated with the original ideas of Franz Roh's post-expressionism and is best discussed under the term 'magic realism'. Many writers in Europe were influenced by the writings of Italian Massimo Bontempelli (1878–1960) who adopted the idea of magic realism from Roh and founded the magazine by the French and Italian speaking '900 Group'. Bontempelli's magic realist fiction and critical essays were written in the 1920s, and varied from more fantastical writing similar to Lewis Carol's *Alice in Wonderland* ([1865] 1929) to his magic realist short stories that explored the 'mysterious and fantastic quality of reality' (Dombroski 1996: 522). Previous to reading Franz Roh, he had been placing emphasis on the function of the imagination and nature in his writing, providing a preparation for the influence of Roh's search for the magic of life shown through the clarity of heightened realism (Dombroski 1996: 522). Although best known for his writing in the 1920s at a time of increasing right-wing political influence that led to the emergence of Mussolini's fascist regime in Italy, he continued to write magic realist works throughout the next two decades, including a piece written in 1943 investigating the meaning of magic realism. Bontempelli thought that magic realism would provide a means to 'de-provincialize' Italian literature and also that it could contribute to Mussolini's unification of Italy by creating a common consciousness. He believed that magic realism in particular provided 'the prime function of a properly modern literature . . . to act on the collective consciousness by opening new mythical and magical perspectives on reality' (Dombroski 1996: 522). During the 1940s and 1960s his writing became the inspiration for the Flemish writers Johan Daisne and Hubert

Lampo. In the 1940s, Johan Daisne (1912–78) regarded Bontempelli's magic realist writing as a form that offered a means to express the distortion of the perception of reality which was the result of the devastation, both physically and psychologically, of Belgium in the wake of two world wars. He recognized that by drawing on this German mode, and incorporating an Italian influence, he could position himself and his writing within an international framework, a stance that was popular in post-war Europe as it was seen to be a means of increasing the chance of lasting peace. His novel *De trap van steen en wolken* (*The Stairs of Stone and Clouds*), written in 1942 during the Second World War, develops magic realism as a means of defining the space between dream and reality; the use of dreams as a source of magic brings his magic realism closer to the surrealism that inspired Roh and German post-expressionism. In what can be seen as a reaction against the horrific experience of the Second World War, Daisne's work is known for its nostalgic treatment of childhood. As critic Michel Dupuis argues, one major source of magic realism for Daisne is the magical perspective of childhood in contrast to the realism of adult reality (1987: 91).

Following Daisne, the younger Flemish writer Hubert Lampo continued a magical realist tradition in Belgium in the 1960s and 1970s. Lampo was also interested in the relationship of dreams to reality, and was influenced by the psychoanalyst Carl Jung's study of the psychology of dreams. Lampo's novels, *De komst van Joachim Stiller* (*The Coming of Joachim Stiller*) ([1960] 1974a) and *Kasper in de onderwereld* (*Kasper in the Underworld*) ([1969] 1974b), like Daisne's, include dream-like narratives but also increase the magic realist aspect by including extraordinary plot coincidences and magical happenings from European myth and fairy tale. For example, in *Kasper in the Underworld*, which is based on the Orpheus and Eurydice myth, the Pied-piper of Hamelin myth is mixed with that of St Francis of Assisi, so that Kasper is able to communicate with animals and they in turn follow him. In this way, Lampo's magic realism, most closely associated with that of Franz Roh and Massimo Bontempelli, is located specifically in Europe through its incorporation of European myths and fairy tales.

The best-known magic realist novel in mainland Europe is *Die Blechtrommel* (*The Tin Drum*) written by the German novelist and Nobel Prize winner Günter Grass in 1959. Grass wrote the novel as a retrospective narrative, looking back to the context of his own early life; he had been brought up in a household that accepted the Nazi propagandists' version of truth, which was overturned at the fall of the Nazi regime at the end of the war. This severely disrupted his perception of reality and prompted him to include a recognizably magical realist account of life under the Nazi regime from the matter-of-fact perspective of a boy, and later, a man, trapped in the body the size of a young child, with an extraordinary capacity for perception. The novel is set in a German-speaking household in a part of Poland that was at the time under German occupation, in the city of Gdansk (then known as Danzig). As Salman Rushdie points out, not only did Grass have his childhood perception of reality overturned at the end of the Second World War, but he also lost his homeland and became a migrant to Berlin (1991: 279). Although Grass himself admits to having been influenced by fairy tales, his magical realism can be seen to have arisen from the same source as García Márquez's; that is, the distortion of truth through the effects of extremely horrific violence, which Grass had witnessed during and immediately after the Second World War (Reder 2000: 75). His literary technique, however, is purposely postmodern, and his narrator adds to the rejection of an absolute truth both through the use of magical realism and through the use of a gleefully unreliable narrator. As well as being playful, Grass's narrator Oskar is also the inmate of an asylum for the mentally ill and so the veracity of his narratives is doubly doubtful. However, all the events of his narrative, whether magical or realist, are presented as the actual truth by Oskar and there is no external commentary to the narrative to signal to the reader to what extent his perception of reality may be disturbed.

Rushdie cites *The Tin Drum* as one of the most influential texts for him whilst writing *Midnight's Children*. In her excellent essay 'Saleem Fathered by Oskar: *Midnight's Children*, Magic Realism and *The Tin Drum*' Patricia Merivale argues that there are many similarities between the two novels, but most important is the fact that Rushdie's 'realization' of metaphors originates from Grass's novel. As Merivale indicates, Oskar's step-father is able to cook his emotions into his soup (a device that is also used in Laura Esquivel's *Like Water for Chocolate*) (1995: 339). Notwithstanding these connections, a discussion of Günter Grass's *The Tin Drum* as an influential magical realist text is problematic. By citing fairy tales as his inspiration for his form of narrative, Grass places his work in relationship with a form of writing that I have already excluded from the category of magical realism, nor does he align himself with Roh, Bontempelli or any other magic realist. In addition, his narrator, as well as being playfully deceptive, is also writing as an inmate in an asylum for the mentally ill. It is for the reader to decide whether or not to trust the narrator and to judge the reliability of his mental state. Can a narrator who is providing a distorted view of reality provide the recognizable realistic elements of the narrative upon which magical realism relies at least in part?

There are two other notable European writers whose work borders on the category of magical realism. In Germany, the writer Patrick Süskind wrote the novel *Das Parfum (Perfume)* ([1985] 1987) in a matter-of-fact narrative supported by minute detail relating the life of a man in eighteenth-century France with no personal scent and an incredibly sensitive sense of smell. The narrative is told from the point of view of the man, Grenouille, who, we soon discover, is attempting to create the most intoxicating scent in the world in order to make people love him. However, his method of producing this scent reveals his inability as a narrator to provide a recognizable and reliable perspective since he is a conscienceless psychopath who murders young women in order to distil their personal scent. In this novel, unlike *The Tin Drum*, we know that we do not share the narrator's perception of reality, and yet the form of the narrative is related to magical realism by its matter-of-fact tone. The fact that the narrator presents his murderous actions to be a part of every-day reality adds to the horror of the novel. The magical realist narrative provides a perfect vehicle to present to the reader the contrast between the psychopath's and the average reader's view of what is ordinary behaviour. The Italian writer Italo Calvino (1923–85) wrote a collection of short stories in a matter-of-fact narrative style which contain extraordinary events. For instance, in '*Il barone rampante*' ('The Baron in the Trees') ([1957] 1980a), a young aristocratic boy refuses to climb down from a tree and remains living there for the rest of his life. However, as Calvino himself states, his stories, like those of Borges, do not rely on a recognizable version of reality to support their magical aspects, but are structured around their own 'internal logic' (1980b: ix). His work is often categorized more simply as postmodern narrative and frequently as meta-fiction, due to the attention given in his narratives to the act of writing, reading and artistic creation.

When we consider the production of magic realist texts in mainland Europe throughout the twentieth century, it becomes clear that Alejo Carpentier's judgement expounded in Chapter 1 was correct: European magic realism remains a narrative mode that is chosen for the purposes of literary experimentation and does not have its source in the writers' mythological and cultural context. Although magic realism originated in Europe it is now more particularly associated with the Latin American form of magical realism and with its associated mythology and cultural context. However, postcolonial and cross-cultural contexts, and particularly those in the English-speaking world, are producing writers who adopt magical realism in order to express their non-Western mythological and cultural traditions. It is these writers who are developing new variations of magical realism that are relevant to their marginalized, postcolonial or cross-cultural contexts. These variations will be explored in detail in the following chapters.

4

TRANSGRESSIVE VARIANTS OF MAGICAL REALISM

Critics considering magical realist fiction have found that it is possible to interpret this narrative mode through various critical and theoretical perspectives. The flexibility of the mode resides in the fact that it is not a genre belonging to one particular era, and therefore is not related to a particular critical approach. However, as this chapter will demonstrate, several critical approaches, which on first consideration may not seem related, in fact are frequently used in relation to magical realist fiction. They are linked in that they all illuminate in different ways the ideas of heterogeneity and multiplicity in modern culture and literature, and perceive this heterogeneity in magical realist fiction. Approaches influenced by theories such as heteroglossia, cross-culturalism, postmodernism and postcolonialism are all shown by many critics to be appropriate to understanding magical realist fiction to such an extent that there are associated 'variants' of magical realism. The following chapters identify these variants separately whilst also indicating the relationship of each of these variants to each other.

The characteristic of magical realism which makes it such a frequently adopted narrative mode is its inherent transgressive and subversive qualities. It is this feature that has led many postcolonial, feminist and cross-cultural writers to embrace it as a means of expressing their ideas. The transgressive and subversive qualities are hinted at in the term itself. The oxymoron 'magical realism' reveals that the categories of the magical and the real are brought into question by their juxtaposition. If in magical realism, as we have established, the magical is presented as a part of ordinary reality, then the distinction between what is magical and what is real is eroded. There are two approaches to understanding how this process comes about. On the one hand, one can claim that magical realism is subversive because it alternates between the real and the magical using the same narrative voice. In this sense, magic remains identifiable as magic and real as real but, unlike in a realist narrative, they are given the same serious treatment. The extent to which one should accept the real as the version of events or the magical as the version of events is continuously undermined by the existence of the other version in the text. On the other hand, one can claim that magical realism is transgressive since magical realism crosses the borders between the magic and real to create a further category – the magical real. This form of magical realism is often discussed by critics in terms of post-structuralist theory which proposes that there are multiple eligible interpretations of a narrative and has become the most frequently adopted approach to magical realism since the 1980s. These theories see the categories defining the difference between the magical and real being dismantled in contemporary culture.

Zamora and Faris have noted both these aspects in their introduction to a collection of essays on magical realism, claiming that such critical analysis reveals that 'Magical realist texts are subversive: their in-between-ness, their all at onceness encourages resistance to monological political and cultural structures, a feature that has made the mode particularly useful to writers in postcolonial cultures and, increasingly, to women' (1995: 6) and that 'magical realism is a mode suited to exploring – and transgressing – boundaries, whether the boundaries are ontological, political, geographical or generic' (1995: 5). They go on to note that the transgressive and subversive aspect of magical realism is very versatile. It can be used, as in the English feminist Angela Carter's writing, to subvert the authority of the British ruling classes or, as in the case of Salman Rushdie, to bring into question the truth of the British version of Indian colonial and postcolonial history. The root of this transgressive and subversive aspect lies in the fact that, once the category of truth has been brought into question and the category of the real broken down or over-turned, the boundaries of other categories become vulnerable. The reader becomes aware that if the category of the real is not definite then all assumptions of truth are also at stake. The post-structuralist critic Kum Kum Sangari, considering the effect of the disruption of boundaries by magical realism, explains that 'The seamless quality of this mode, the difficulty of distinguishing between fact and invention, brings an enormous pressure to bear upon the perception of reality' (1987: 162).

Most critics of magical realism, like Sangari, and the majority of writers of magical realism understand the world to be ruled and controlled by a predominantly male and white Western elite. Predominantly, they have been influenced by the ideas of Karl Marx or by the feminist theories of Simone de Beauvoir in the mid-twentieth century or the postcolonial writers such as Frantz Fanon and Edward Said in the middle to latter part of the twentieth century. The critics of magical realism often express their understanding of the concept in terms of cultural conflict between the dominant ruling classes and those who have been denied power. The vocabulary of 'otherness' is frequently employed to refer to those who have been denied power. In colonial terms it is understood that it is the political power to govern oneself but also the power to define the world around you that has been denied the 'others'. In the case of the United States, the dominant culture is assumed to be that of the male Anglo-European population who have governed the country since its independence. In the United Kingdom it is assumed to be the males of the 'ruling upper class'. Both of these dominant cultures promote attitudes that can be traced to the Enlightenment period of colonialist eighteenth-century Britain and America. These ideas assumed that all truth could be known through logic and science without the need for the superstitions of religion. The image of the American entrepreneur and politician Benjamin Franklin attempting to arrange his life through logically and practically drawn schedules is a characteristic, if somewhat ridiculous, image of an Enlightenment man. Charles Darwin's explanation for the evolution of man from amphibians rather than from God is a central and typically scientifically based theory of the Enlightenment. In broader terms, their quest for truth through logical thinking, and the assumption that they had the correct means to find it, meant that the notion of truth and what is true came to be defined by these powerful men. The dominant culture remained dominant by denying others the power to govern and the power to challenge the truths that they proposed.

When we consider magical realism from the position of the 'other' and consider that it brings into view non-logical and non-scientific explanations for things, we can see that the transgressive power of magical realism provides a means to attack the assumptions of the dominant culture and particularly the notion of scientifically and logically determined truth. In effect, as Zamora and Faris note, magical realism brings into question the very assumptions of dominant culture and the influential ideas of the Enlightenment (1995: 6).

No one writer attacks the authority of the male British ruling classes and their dominant culture more adeptly than the feminist Angela Carter. Using magical realism as her means of attack, particularly in her novel *Wise Children* ([1991] 1992), her characters subvert the authority of the patriarchal upper class by emphasizing to excess the attributes of the female, illegitimate working class. Following the post-structuralist feminist theories of Hélène Cixous, it is understood that dominant patriarchal authority defines itself in opposition to the 'other', and in this case, the female. Cixous clarifies this situation by revealing the logic of European languages, in which nouns and adjectives frequently divide into opposite pairs – the one negative and the other positive (1989: 102). This feminist argument asserts that patriarchal authority defines women by making all assumed female attributes negative as opposed to the positive male attributes. This would include, for instance, in our case, the binary oppositions of superstition versus rationalism. Carter's novel is structured around such pairings. The novel follows the story of two music hall dancers who are the illegitimate and unacknowledged twin daughters of a high-cultured Shakespearean actor. They live in a dreary part of South London with his wheel-chair-bound previous wife, whereas he lives in an exclusive part of North London with his new family. He is acclaimed whereas they are forgotten. They are raucous and crude with language, preferring to speak in slang, whereas he is an orator and speaks with precision, perfect elocution and sophisticated vocabulary. Although they are all elderly, the twins insist on accentuating their sensuality by the clothes that they wear, going against the patriarchal idea that older women are no longer sexually attractive or active. In fact, they disrupt more than one party by having such active sex that it almost destroys the buildings around them. The magical realism in the novel is a mixture of excessive acts such as catastrophic sex, their excessive liveliness in older age and conjuring acts that come true such as a missing girl appearing from a box. The climax of the novel sees the twins attending their father's one-hundredth birthday celebration where they create havoc by declaring their parentage to the public. This intentionally subversive act reveals the inter-relatedness of the illegitimate to the legitimate, the working class to the upper class, the female to the male, and the low culture to the high culture. By placing her emphasis on the female, working class, illegitimate and popular, and revealing the fragility of borders between the two opposing worlds, Carter turns the system of binary oppositions upside down and brings into question the assumptions of such patriarchal definitions.

Angela Carter's novels are widely recognized as being indebted to the Russian critic Mikhail Bakhtin's (1895–1975) theories of the carnivalesque and heteroglossia in the novel. The magical realist critic Brenda Cooper also notes that since magical realism has become popular in the second half of the twentieth century, the usefulness of Bakhtin's theories in relation to the concept has become increasingly acknowledged (1998: 23). Bakhtin studied the revolutionary effects of the traditional form of carnival in which those deprived of power enacted the roles of those with power, such as a donkey being cast as a priest. This, combined with the lack of control and exuberance of a festive atmosphere, provides the occasion for the disempowered to express their opposition to the system under which they live. By reversing the binary oppositions and allowing her characters to express such a festive exuberance, Carter's work epitomizes Bakhtin's idea of the carnivalesque in literature. Her magical realism also plays its part in creating this carnivalesque atmosphere, as it relies upon a reversal of categories in which the magical becomes real and the real becomes magical. In addition, much of this exuberance can be articulated in literature through the expression of multiple perspectives in a single novel. Bakhtin noted the importance in modern novels of polyphony, or multiple and conflicting voices, which he called 'heteroglossia'. Again, this can be seen as the expression of both magical and realist perspectives in magical realist texts. When we compare the definitions of magical realism cited in the introduction with the description of Bakhtin's carnivalesque in Peter Stallybrass and Allon White's *The Politics and Poetics of Transgression* (1986), it becomes apparent that there is a close relationship between the concepts because carnivalesque is 'a world of topsy-turvy, of heteroglot exuberance, of ceaseless overrunning and excess, where all is mixed, hybrid, ritually degraded and defiled' (1986: 8). In fact, in her novel *Wise Children* Carter proposes that it is the elements of transgression and excess in carnival that allow illusion to work and the improbable to become possible.

The Indian critic Kum Kum Sangari proposes that the magical realist attack on dominant culture and its authoritative version of the truth actually provides a new and more 'comprehensive mode of referentiality' (1987: 163). By this she means that it provides a new way of understanding categories without having to rely on absolute truth or fixed definitions. This point of view is shared by many critics of magical realism who recognize that by breaking down the notion of an absolute truth, and a singular version of reality, magical realism allows for the possibility of many truths to exist simultaneously. It is for this reason that Isabel Allende chose this mode of fiction for her first novel *The House of the Spirits* ([1982] 1986), and is one of the predominant reasons why the Chinese American writer Maxine Hong Kingston adopted magical realism for her semi-autobiographical novel *The Woman Warrior* ([1976] 1981a). Both women, in different contexts, were unable to express their own, or their community's, version of the truth of their histories or lives due to the oppressive authority of both the government and the patriarchal environment in which they lived.

Isabel Allende is famously related to the previous president Salvador Allende of Chile who was ousted from power in a coup in 1973. This coup brought to power the notorious right-wing government led by Augusto Pinochet. Allende's novel *The House of the Spirits* follows this turbulent time in Chile's history from the point of view of the women of the household of a ruling-class family. The novel portrays Chile descending into a horrific situation, and clearly positions itself against the final coup of the right-wing government, which can be interpreted as that of Pinochet. Allende, as a relative of Salvador Allende and a journalist and writer against the Pinochet government, which was notorious for suspected 'disappearances' (assassinations of people whose bodies have never been found) and imprisonment of political opposition, was warned against remaining in Chile and has lived in exile in Venezuela and the United States for most of her adult life. In this delicately political and threatening situation, the novel employs magical realism for multiple subversive effects. First, the magical realist events of the novel, such as the telepathy of the character Clara, emphasize that it is fiction. In this way, the evidently political content of the novel is placed in a clearly fictional context, which undermines a reading of the novel as direct political commentary against the Pinochet government. However, Allende uses the paradoxical aspect of magical realism also to claim that the magical aspects of her novel, such as the clairvoyance, are the true characteristics of her own grandmother and mother (Hart 1989: 56). In addition, by Allende's own admission, the novel is based on her family history and she acknowledges that Salvador Allende is the role model for her character of *el Presidente* who is also ousted in a coup (Price 1990: 69). These conflicting messages undermine each other and produce a confusing context with which to approach the text. This is magical realism at work.

The reference to clairvoyance in this magical realist novel is not haphazard. In fact, Patricia Hart notes that it is linked to the political situation of Chile under the Pinochet government. Hart notes that Allende emphasizes the fact that the right-wing dictatorship in her novel attempts to manipulate the population by fearful predictions of the future and political failure. She explains that 'Within the world of *la casa de los espíritus* the Left torments itself over failure to foresee the coup d'état, while the Right continues to use clairvoyant arguments to justify brutality (i.e. the coup was necessary because without it *el Presidente* would have declared himself President-for-Life and a civil war would have erupted)' (Hart 1989: 66). In this way, Hart proposes that the ability of the women of the novel to predict the future reveals the fraudulence of the government's claims and undermines its influence over the people.

Of course, Allende's continued life in exile is proof that it cannot be assumed that the use of magical realism to confuse the boundary between reality and fiction in this overtly political novel disguised its thinly veiled attack of the Pinochet government. In fact, many critics see that the use of magical realism in the novel weakens its political content. Allende has claimed that she wanted *The House of the Spirits* to have a similar spirit to that of the writing of the Caribbean region of Latin America, which she describes as the 'mixture of joy and disorder' (Price 1990: 66). This, of course, is the region and the atmosphere of the works of García Márquez and it has often been noted that Allende's *The House of the Spirits* owes a lot to *One Hundred Years of Solitude*, including the use of a narrator who constructs the narrative from reclaimed books. This provides an explanation for why many of the magical realist incidents are trivialized by the reaction of the characters who matter-of-factly avoid minor problems by using their clairvoyant skills. But the use of magical realism notably lessens towards the end of the novel and, in fact, decreases with increased political violence. Patricia Hart explains that this a complex ploy by Allende for feminist purposes. She argues that the magical realism in *The House of the Spirits* is associated only with the women of the novel and lessens with the domination of the male world of political violence in Chile. However, she also notes that the magical qualities of the female characters are purposefully undermined in the novel. Arguing that it is a form of feminist criticism of the patriarchal control over the women's lives that she calls 'magical feminism', Hart claims that the women find other sources of power, such as telepathy, in the absence of access to any other real power (1989: 54). When Alba, the granddaughter and narrator, is able to join the fight against the government through direct political action, she does not use any magical powers and in fact ignores a prediction that she will be harmed, which comes true when she is captured and tortured. Hart explains that:

> Magic is alternately used or withheld to make a point about the economic and emotional dependence of women at certain time periods. The fact that Blanca and Clara are unable to liberate themselves from passivity and manipulation is hardly a criticism of Allende's own feminism; rather it is a tribute to her honesty as a novelist.
>
> (1989: 54)

The critic Philip Swanson interprets this differently, thinking back to Alba's lack of power when she is tortured, and claims that:

> Clara's spiritualism, on one level, simply represents happy times which are destroyed by natural and political cataclysms. The world of the

spirits, in other words, is the sort of ideal place the world should be. In the meantime, the positive force of Clara's spiritualism needs to be harnessed on a practical and political level.

(1995: 163)

The future for Alba and for Chile are left open at the end, but with the positive note that Alba has the resources to incorporate her grandmother's gifts as she has also inherited her notebooks.

The writing of Chinese American Maxine Hong Kingston, although also subversive and feminist, is less overtly political than Allende's. All the same, the novel *The Woman Warrior: Memoir of a Girlhood Among Ghosts* attempts to subvert both the subtle patriarchal and governmental control over the lives of Chinese American women. The narrator, the daughter of immigrant parents from mainland China growing up in California in the mid-twentieth century is in need of a sense of her own worth and identity. She feels unsure of her value as a female in her community due to the misogynist stories and proverbs that she hears, and is uncertain of the extent to which she is required to adopt Chinese traditions, due to a lack of parental guidance in these matters. Being from a community that was highly restricted by immigration controls, she is unable to ask direct questions about her family's previous life in China and is unsure of the truth of what she is told. As entrance to the United States often relied on having a living relative already in the country, many families created and memorized false family trees, even entire fictional villages, in order to be allowed to land. The men who arrived under such circumstance were known as 'paper sons'. The Asian American critic Gayle K. Fujito Sato comments that:

> The strategy of 'paper sons' meant that from the start the Chinese were authoring their American lives, that notions of 'real' identity were never uncomplicated. Folklore and fantasy in the creation of self were implicit in the very beginning of Chinese American society.
>
> (1991: 199)

The narrator's only sources of information are these stories and the stories that her mother tells her. She initially complains to her mother that 'I can't tell what's real and what you make up' (Hong Kingston 1981a:

180). In this and many other ways *The Woman Warrior* is a novel about magical realism and is overtly about finding the difference between the 'real' and the 'fake' aspects of Chinese culture with which the heroine is confronted. The narrator's growing-up process is one by which she manages to accept the fictional aspect of her own reality and to use it to create a sense of who she is and what her context is. She eventually adapts one of her mother's stories about a Chinese woman living amongst barbarians to create a mythical version of her own cross-cultural situation in America.

On another level, the novel relies upon magical realism to emphasize that the contents are fictional in order to protect it from being used as proof either against her family by the community or against any member of the community by the immigration authorities. The novel begins by setting forward the two problems which the narrator must negotiate in her quest to understand and create her own identity. Her mother tells her of a taboo story about an aunt who commits suicide due to the shame she brings onto the family by becoming pregnant through adultery. In the opening line of the novel the mother tells the young narrator about the aunt who is known as 'no name woman', saying: "'You must not tell anyone"... "what I am about to tell you'" (Hong Kingston 1981a: 11). The narrator needs to negotiate both the threat of breaking a taboo by writing her autobiography, and also of bringing shame to her family by repeating her aunt's story. She fears becoming a woman with no name, rejected by her family and community for breaking the taboos. Her mother ends her story warning that 'The villagers are watchful' and the young narrator notices that indeed they are vigilant, she has even witnessed them ejecting a woman from their community (Hong Kingston 1981a: 13). By adapting the myths of China told to her by her mother and repeating her mother's magical realist ghost tales in order to create her own story, she undermines the more realistic autobiographical aspects of her novel and avoids any assumption that what she has written is provable or true.

Ultimately, Hong Kingston has attempted and succeeded in protecting sensitive information about her family's and community's immigration status by writing a novel in which the magical realist elements undermine the idea that the autobiographical details are true while allowing them to remain realistic.

However, as has been witnessed in relation to the *fatwa* imposed by the Ayatollah Khomeini on Salman Rushdie after he published *The Satanic Verses* in 1989 for insulting Islam, the assumption that because a book emphasizes its fictionality by using magical realism and can thus be exonerated from political control is dangerous and can sometimes be simply wrong. As Timothy Brennan notices, from some critical perspectives Rushdie's book can be seen as a 'parody of Mohammed's life' (1989: 144). For some, even if the parody is in the form of fiction, it is still an act of heresy. Also, Isabel Allende's magical realism did not protect her from a prolonged exile from Chile during the Pinochet regime. It can be said that whilst magical realism can be used to subvert authority, its fictionality cannot protect it from causing offence by its overtly purposeful coincidences.

POSTMODERNIST MAGICAL REALISM

Postmodernism is one of the few terms more difficult to define than magical realism. For the purposes of considering postmodernism's relationship to magical realism, it is better to allow multiple, and sometimes conflicting, definitions to be borne in mind. Two theorists in particular provide a useful means of considering some of the more recent magical realism writing as postmodernist. These theorists, Fredric Jameson and Jean-François Lyotard (1924–98), writing in the last three decades of the twentieth century, provide definitions of postmodernism that accentuate the importance of history and the need to find ways to represent that which so far has been beyond ordinary discourse.

In his *Postmodernism or, The Cultural Logic of Late Capitalism* (1991), Fredric Jameson claims that postmodernism is the 'attempt to think the present historically in an age that has forgotten how to think historically in the first place' (1991: 3). Although the extent to which historical references appear in magical realist writing may seem to indicate that magical realists have not forgotten how to think historically, we need to examine the way in which historical references and attempts at historical revision occur in magical realist works in order to gain an understanding of the relationship between magical realism and postmodernism. As we have seen, many magical realist works include historical references, not only to situate their texts in a particular context, but also to bring into question already existing historical assumptions. In fact, postmodernist thinking about history usually emphasizes the lack of absolute historical truth and casts doubt over the existence of fact by indicating its link with narrative and stories. A typical postmodernist view of history is that of Elizabeth Tonkin who writes that histories are 'arguments created by people in particular conditions' (1990: 18). Following Jameson's Marxist stance, it is understood that versions of history that claim to be the only truth are usually created by people in power in order to justify their position and maintain it. For this reason, such an approach to history and postmodernism is frequently adopted by postcolonial magical realist writers. Salman Rushdie's writing, and in particular *Midnight's Children*, provides us with perfectly illustrative examples of how magical realism can work with this form of historical postmodernism. In his essays on writing, *Imaginary Homelands*, Rushdie reflects the views of Jameson and Tonkin, stating that 'History is always ambiguous. Facts are hard to establish, and capable of being given many meanings. Reality is built on prejudices, misconceptions and ignorance as well as on our perceptiveness and knowledge' (1991: 25).

Rushdie reached this point of understanding through the process of writing *Midnight's Children*. In this novel he retraces the Bombay and India of his own childhood not as autobiography but as cultural history. The history he provides is not that written in colonial history books, but is one constructed around individuals and their involvement in the historical process, such as a character's unwitting involvement in the Amritsar massacre of 1919 carried out by the British forces. More significantly, the main character of the novel, Saleem, is a child and later an adult protagonist who was born at exactly the same time that India as a nation came into being as an independent state. As Saleem comments, he had been 'mysteriously handcuffed to history, my destinies indissolubly chained to those of my country' (1982: 9). Therefore, if we recall Jameson's definition of postmodernism, we can see that Saleem himself is being forced to think historically through the circumstances of his birth at a time when the country of India is leaving its colonial history behind and forming its own national identity. However, having attempted to recreate the past in his mind, Rushdie found that his memory was unreliable and any history that he created would be equally so. Rather than dismiss history or attempt to enforce an authoritarian version of historical truth in his novel, Rushdie embraces the very postmodern aspect of attempting to recreate history with fragments and uncertainty. Commenting in conversation with Jean-Pierre Durix, he explains: 'I found that I did not have total recall about the past, that I was only remembering certain things very vividly, sometimes accurately and sometimes not, they became much more powerful, as though they were bits of archaeological remains' (1998: 12).

In fact, Rushdie's work illustrates that, if history is to be seen from each individual's perspective, in order to get close to providing a comprehensive portrayal of India, he must acknowledge the multiplicity of historical perspectives and give equal validity to each one. It is through this portrayal of multiple perspectives that Rushdie most closely associates his magical realist narrative with a postmodern approach to history. His character Saleem, the narrator of the story and so the purveyor of this postmodern version of history, admits that:

> there are so many stories to tell, too many, such an excess of inter-twined lives events miracle places rumours, so dense a commingling of the improbable and the mundane! I have been a swallower of lives; and to know me, just the one of me, you'll have to swallow the lot as well.
>
> (1982: 9)

In other words, if all perspectives are to be articulated with the same validity then they will include contradictory perspectives, such as the magical and the realist, which will be given equal weight by the narrative.

In an essay exploring the notion of history in *Midnight's Children*, Neil Ten Kortenaar comments that 'Rushdie's novel is a meditation on the textuality of history' (1995: 42). This is very much the case if we consider that the narrative of *Midnight's Children*, which follows the history of India through the impressions of Saleem and his own stories of his ancestors, is written by the older Saleem in a pickle factory and with great self-reflexivity. Saleem includes himself as writer in his narratives, setting the scene by presenting himself 'While I sit like an empty pickle jar in a pool of Anglepoised light, visited by this vision of my grandfather sixty-three years ago, which demands to be recorded' (1982: 19). A recurring image of his writing created by Saleem that is present here is his attempt to 'pickle history' and store it in a jar. As the end of the novel approaches not only is Saleem, the person who shares his fate with his country, beginning to disintegrate in much the same way as India, but his pickle jars are leaking. The attempt to preserve and maintain order with historical fact has failed and the juices from all the various jars mingle together, uncontained. Ten Kortenaar interprets this to indicate that *Midnight's Children* both undermines and presumes the possibility of history, and it does so in order to encourage a self-reflexiveness in the reader' (1995: 56).

If we consider that the inclusion of magical realism itself in a text provokes the reader to reflect on what they are willing to believe and on their own assumptions about reality, this revelation of the constructed nature of history demands a double self-reflexivity from the reader and on the part of the narrative. Working with similar terms to Jameson but with less emphasis on a Marxist perspective, the theorist Linda Hutcheon claims that postmodernism is the 'ironic reworking of the past' and that it 'works with the very systems it attempts to subvert' (1988: 4). She, like Neil Ten Kortenaar, emphasizes the self-reflexivity of postmodernist fiction. Her book *A Poetics of Postmodernism* (1988) is an examination of exactly the kind of text exemplified by *Midnight's Children*. She considers the link between self-reflexivity and the inclusion of historical fact in late twentieth-century fiction and names this kind of narrative 'historiographic metafiction'. She includes Rushdie's *Midnight's Children* and García Márquez's *One Hundred Years of Solitude* as prime examples of this kind of fiction and notes that 'its theoretical self-awareness of history and fiction as human constructs . . . is made the grounds for its rethinking of the form and contents of the past' (Hutcheon 1988: 5).

One Hundred Years of Solitude is indeed an attempt to recreate history and to bring into question those historical 'facts' which have been incorporated into official versions of history. Whether García Márquez's novel serves as a history of Colombia or more broadly as a history of Latin America is disputed by critics. Stephen Minta sees the novel as pertinent to both and claims 'He is . . . inevitably concerned with the whole history of his country and continent, and . . . he has constantly laid stress on the importance of developing alternative sources of history as a challenge to the status of conventional ones' (1987: 30). His alternative sources of history are the manuscripts of Melquíades which tell the family story of the Buendías and through them tell the story of forgotten incidents in the rural and isolated setting of Macondo. The fictional story of the Buendías includes actual historical events such as a strike on a banana plantation in the region in 1928 which ended in violence (Williams 1985: 6).

Patricia Merivale notes that the structure of *One Hundred Years of Solitude* itself includes two approaches to the same stories. One approach is the chronological plot of the history of the Buendía family in Macondo. This contrasts with the second approach that consists of fragmented and non-chronological records of the same events in the manuscripts of Melquíades. Merivale points out that the difference in the treatment of time in the two versions creates a tension in the text between the linear narrative of the family history and the cyclical narrative of the manuscripts (1995: 330). However, as the reader is only made aware of Melquíades's manuscripts by the chronological narrative of the family, the linear narrative is not greatly disrupted by Melquíades. This double narrative structure introduces a self-reflexive element to the narration which makes the reader aware that the narrator is conscious of the way in which the narrative is constructed.

The critic Kum Kum Sangari considers that this self-reflexive aspect of *One Hundred Years of Solitude* goes hand-in-hand with magical realism in order to disrupt fixed notions of history. According to Sangari, by revealing its constructedness and making knowledge and truth 'provisional', such novels as *One Hundred Years of Solitude* revise history to make it relevant to the present circumstance (1987: 163). This is, in effect, another way of proposing Jameson's definition of postmodernism – to think historically in an age when authoritative history is forgotten or mistrusted.

This is very much the case with the novel *Beloved* ([1987] 1988) by Toni Morrison. Morrison has stated that to forget the past leads to spiritual and cultural emptiness (Evans 1985: 344). She claims that she wrote the novel *Beloved*, which is an attempt to recover the stories of slavery from the point of view of female slaves and their offspring, in order to remind African Americans of their past. She hoped, by doing so, to gain recognition of the injustice, and for African Americans to confront and move on from the pain of the slavery period and its aftermath. She uses the magical realist device of a revenant ghost child in full bodily form to bring back the memories of the heavily traumatized escaped slave Sethe, who while under threat of re-capture, kills her baby in order to protect her. The pain of such a past means that Sethe is reluctant to think of it and is unable to tell her surviving daughter about the past. The remaining daughter, Denver, with the help of the revenant Beloved, draws out Sethe's stories so that together they can go through a process of healing. They create history themselves by telling stories to each other made up from the fragments of the past that they have been able to glean. Ultimately, Denver is able to move on from her childhood and take her place in the wider world. The revenant Beloved returns to the water where she came from and leaves only footprints that change shape depending on the foot-size of the person who places their own foot in them. In this way, Beloved becomes symbolic of all women who were enslaved. She is also symbolic of all the women who are 'under the water', drowned or thrown dead overboard in the Atlantic during the middle-crossing journey on the slave ships from Africa, to whom Morrison dedicates her novel. Their story stands in opposition to the official history of white slave owners which has silenced many horrific personal histories of slaves in the United States. Morrison's postmodern novel is not so much an attempt to think historically in an age that does not know how, so much as an attempt to think historically from a historical perspective that has been silenced.

Morrison's novel can be seen to support Jean-François Lyotard's notion of postmodernism. Written in 1979, his study *The Postmodern Condition: A Report on Knowledge* works from the premise that modernism created a splintering of life from art. Lyotard claims that in the postmodern age we need a broader inclusion of life experience in art. His ultimate statement concerning postmodernism is that it 'puts forward the unrepresentable in presentation itself' (Lyotard 1984: 81).

As it is unavoidable to express onseself in the vocabulary of dominant discourse, Morrison's stories that are told from the perspective of women slaves are indeed unrepresentable. Morrison creates a history for such women by using magical realism to express the 'real' that is 'beyond language' in stories. When Lyotard requests 'Let us wage war on totality; let us be witnesses to the unrepresentable; let us activate the differences' (1984: 82) he seems to be almost speaking directly to magical realist texts by writers such as García Márquez, Rushdie and Morrison. All three writers 'wage war on totality' by using magical realist devices to disrupt fixed categories of truth, reality and history. Their multiple-perspectived texts and the disruption of categories create a space beyond authoritative discourse where the unrepresentable can be expressed.

5

CROSS-CULTURAL VARIANTS
OF MAGICAL REALISM

The oxymoron that makes up the term magical realism provides a structure for this mode of writing that includes opposing or contradictory points of view. The vocabulary used to describe this polarity at the heart of magical realism often indicates opposing worlds or at the very least, world views. Geoff Hancock, for instance, describes magic realism as constituting the 'conjunction of two worlds' (1980: 7) – the magical and the realist. Likewise, Amaryll Chanady states that magical realism is an 'amalgamation of a rational and an irrational world view' (1985: 21). Lois Zamora and Wendy Faris observe that the conjunction or amalgamation of these two worlds creates a mixture of these opposing cultures, and a third space, which is constituted from neither one nor the other of the opposing world views, but from the creation of a third which gives equal credence to the influence of the other two: 'The propensity of magical realist texts to admit a plurality of worlds means that they often situate themselves on liminal territory between or among these worlds' (1995: 6). It is not surprising then to find that many writers whose cultural perspectives include varied and sometimes contradictory cultural influences are drawn to magical realism as a form of expression.

Even as early as the beginnings of magical realist writing in Latin America by Alejo Carpentier and Miguel Asturias, the cross-cultural nature of Latin America and the suitability of magical realism to express this aspect was emphasized. Carpentier calls this the '*mestizaje*' (culturally and racially mixed) aspect of Latin American culture (1995b: 100). He refers in particular to the different cultural influences provided by the African American and the indigenous people of Latin America. Even today this mixture of cultural influences is seen to provide the distinct characteristics of Latin America for writers such as Isabel Allende. Following Carpentier's belief that magical realism is specifically Latin American, she explains that it 'relies on a South American reality: the confluence of races and cultures of the whole world superimposed on the indigenous culture, in a violent climate' (Foreman 1995: 286).

Magical realism is often criticized for relying on a European viewpoint that assumes that magic and the irrational belong to indigenous and non-European cultures, whereas rationality and a true sense of reality belong to a European perspective. Carpentier, Allende and Chanady all seem to suggest this in the previous quotations, which leads to the accusation that they are repeating the colonialist attitudes established by the European Enlightenment in which reason, rationality, and science were considered to be the means to reveal the truth: non-European people, it was assumed through racial prejudice, were incapable of such thought and therefore of knowing the 'truth'. This will be discussed in more detail in relation to the critic Liam Connell in the final chapter. In a sense, it is unfair to make these accusations against Allende, based on this one statement, with the same force as those made against Carpentier. Carpentier based his novels on these ideas whereas we have seen that Allende's writing refers to a more Christian and European form of spiritualism and magic and she does not borrow from the myths of the indigenous population or assume that they are irrational. Moreover, Allende's use of the word 'superimposed' in her quotation recognizes the colonialist effect of settlers in Latin America on the indigenous population.

In recent English language magical realism, the dangers of including colonial racial assumptions have been lessened by the predominance of writing from the cross-cultural perspective of a narrator who possesses a predominantly non-European or non-Western cultural perspective. There has been a proliferation of writers in cross-cultural contexts who, in the words of Zamora and Faris, 'self-consciously recuperate non-Western cultural modes and non-literary forms in the Western form (the novel)' (1995: 4). Writers such as Toni Morrison, Maxine Hong Kingston and Leslie Marmon Silko, writing during the last three decades of the twentieth century in the United States from three different American perspectives, each adopted the narrative device of magical realism. Although Morrison has acknowledged that she uses the technique, she, Hong Kingston and Silko have all since rejected the term due to misconceptions brought about by the overly frequent use of the term in the 1990s. However, they employed the narrative technique of magical realism in order to express their own personal interpretations of their cross-cultural contexts in the face of domination by European American culture.

As they each explain, their cultural contexts include influences from dominant American culture (including their adoption of the originally European form of the novel) but also from their alternative cultural communities – the African Americans, Chinese Americans and Native Americans – all of whom have been persecuted by European Americans. Their aim is to challenge the dominant culture's authority and thereby lessen its power in order to articulate their communal histories which provide the necessary knowledge for establishing and articulating their cultural identities. As a part of this persecution and domination by European Americans, the histories of their persecution remained untold or told with the bias of European Americans for many decades. The Native American writer Simon Ortiz explains the difference of approach to history of European 'Westernized' Americans and his own community; 'History is the experience we live. I suppose "history" in the Western definition means something that is really a kind of contrived information to support the present case, the present United States' existence and aims' (Bruchac 1987: 223). Toni Morrison notes that the history of the slavery of African Americans from their own perspective has remained untold due to the oversight of dominant American (and previously slave-owning) culture. She claims:

> We live in a land where the past is always erased and America is the innocent future in which immigrants can come and start over . . . The

> culture doesn't encourage dwelling on, let alone coming to terms with, the truth about the past.
>
> (Ferguson 1991: 189)

Morrison claims that magical realism provides 'Another way of knowing things' (Evans 1985: 342). This other way, which in her words blends the two worlds of practicality and magic together, allows the expression of a story that goes against what 'authoritative' history from a European American perspective claims. It also allows for the expression of African American myths that do not originate from European American culture, and for the expression of such myths that makes them approachable and meaningful for African Americans in a modern context.

For this reason Morrison's novels such as *Beloved* and *Song of Solomon* are set in an African American community at a particular historical moment. The central characters, Sethe and Denver in *Beloved* and Milkman in *Song of Solomon*, are searching for a way to understand their family's and their community's past. Morrison acknowledges that her aim in constructing narratives of African American history is an attempt to create a cultural memory for African Americans so that they can have a sense of how they became who they are today and what their past achievements had been. A large part of this creation of a cultural memory is the expression of a specifically African American culture. Using aspects of African American oral culture and myths that evolved during the time of slavery and are traceable today, some of which refer back to a West African cultural heritage, Morrison weaves African American cultural traits into her novels, which are also influenced by European American writers such as William Faulkner, and so creates a new cross-cultural context. Morrison's most famous magical realist happenings in her novel are in *Beloved*, the appearance in full bodily form of a girl who is understood to be Sethe's dead baby Beloved, who was killed by Sethe in order to save her from slave catchers and, in *Song of Solomon*, the flight of Milkman as he dies after having traced his family to the patriarch of Solomon the flying African. The appearance of Beloved can be interpreted as both that of a revenant ghost, that is an apparition in full bodily form, or as an *abiku* child, which is a child from West African Yoruba mythology who returns from the dead to be born again to the same mother. The story of Milkman can be interpreted as the Icarus myth but it is more convincing as the retelling of African American folklore which claims that when slaves died they returned to Africa by flying across the sea. Both of these myths can be found in differing forms in Ben Okri's Nigerian magical realist novel *The Famished Road* in which Azaro is also an *abiku* child caught between the worlds of the dead and the living, and in Alejo Carpentier's *The Kingdom of this World* in which the rebel slave Mackandal flies away when he dies.

Leslie Marmon Silko's *Almanac of the Dead* ([1991] 1992) is a complex novel with over fifty characters and differing settings. However, the central thrust of the novel is a call for environmental change and a consideration of Native American cultural beliefs which prioritize the wellbeing of the earth. Although there are many characters from differing cultural backgrounds whose stories are told in the novel, the overarching perspective of the novel is Native American. It is an expression of a point of view of a cultural group who are still under the colonial power of European Americans, who, between the eighteenth and mid-twentieth century killed many Native Americans, claimed their lands from them and organized them to live on reservations. Silko's text, however, is also a novel which draws on the fiction of postmodernist Californian Thomas Pynchon, among other European Americans, for literary inspiration and is set amongst characters of all nationalities in urban centres such as San Diego. This creates a strongly oppositional cross-culturalism in which the differing cultural influences are directly contradictory. In order to express both elements without one cancelling the other, her text relies heavily on the use of a magical realist narrative mode in order for the Native American myths to be accepted on the same level as recognizable American reality. The main source of Silko's magical realist plots is Native Mexican cultural practices, including the belief in the macaw as a sacred bird and the use of prayer bundles for guidance. The character Tacho, who becomes a leader of an environmental movement against the destruction of the earth by present-day Americans, talks to the macaws and asks them for advice. However, it is more the manner in which the Native American beliefs of the living character of the earth and the relatedness of all living things are placed in the text as a matter of fact that provides the alternative perspective from that of everyday American reality as perceived by the dominant culture. For instance, the fragment of the ancient Mayan Almanacs that is referred to in the title is transcribed and interpreted to provide a prophecy of the salvation of the earth by Tacho and his twin which is being set in motion during the action of the novel. The prophecy claims that they will arrive from the direction indicated by the great snake in the hills. This prophecy is based on two existing Laguna Pueblo Native American myths. The first is the emergence myth of the Laguna Pueblo that claims that the earth began when a pair of twins led the people into the present world and the second myth is that of the carved stone snake at the mine of Paguate which was discovered in 1979 and is believed to have special powers (Silko 1997: 126). The radical cross-culturalism of this novel and its magical realism resides in the fact that these Native American beliefs are proposed to the reader during the reading of the novel but are also intended to be considered after reading, no matter what the cultural background of the reader.

Maxine Hong Kingston's novels *The Woman Warrior: Memoirs of a Girlhood Among Ghosts* ([1976] 1981a), *China Men* ([1980] 1981b) and *Tripmaster Monkey: His Fake Book* ([1989] 1990), like Morrison's, are written in order to express the history of her community and, in Hong Kingston's case, to create a cultural memory for the Chinese American community. As a group they were subjected to prolonged racist immigration restrictions until 1948. Chinese women were prohibited from entering the United States in a bid to stop them settling as a group and having families in the country. This led to a culture of secrecy in order to guard against exposure to the authorities who might find evidence of illegal entry into the United States. False family histories were common, resulting in the confusion of later generations in relation to their ancestry. Hong Kingston's *The Woman Warrior* is semi-autobiographical and includes her anger at her parents for her lack of understanding of her Chinese heritage. As well as being confused by the secrecy surrounding her family history, the young narrator finds her mother's magical realist stories of China confusing in the extreme. She accuses her mother of 'lying' with stories (1981a: 180). One of her mother's most magical realist tales tells of how she battled with a ghost in a dormitory at her medical school. The detailed description and categorization of what kind of ghost it was combined with the description of the medical school where the mother learnt scientifically based medicine and rejected folkloric cures creates a magical tale told in the context of rationalism. However, this magical realism is entirely set in China and it is notable that it is the narrator's American perspective which provides the cross-cultural aspect to the text whereas the magic remains in China and in a cultural context unfamiliar to the narrator. Ghosts proliferate in Hong Kingston's work, although in the United States the word 'ghost' is simply used by the Chinese characters to refer to anybody who is not Chinese. The young narrator, being in a state of confusion, does not understand this and so is perpetually terrified. This emphasizes the magical realist aspect for the narrator, although it is not due to a specific magical happening but arises, rather, from the narrator's confusion about what is real and what is not real, about what is a ghost and what is not a ghost. The effort in her novels to untangle what it means to her to be a Chinese American is part of a broader attempt to provide a cultural memory for Chinese Americans. The use of magical realism for such a novel not only portrays the confusion between the categories of the real and the fake, or the real and the magical, but also brings into question what constitutes a multiply influenced culture such as the Chinese American.

In the context of the discussion of the cultural positioning of magical realism, it is notable that many of the novelists mentioned in this book draw on non-European cultural influences from orally transmitted myths. These myths often include magical elements that do not follow realist or rational lines. The magical aspects of their work, therefore, appear to come from non-European influences set against the dominant culture's rational, realist context. However, to contend with the criticism set out at the beginning of this section, Zamora and Faris point out that:

> Texts labelled magical realist draw upon cultural systems that are no less 'real' than those upon which traditional literary realism draws – often non-Western cultural systems that privilege mystery over empiricism, empathy over technology, tradition over innovation. Their primary narrative investment may be in myths, legends, ritual – that is in collective (sometimes oral and performative, as well as written) practices that bind communities together.
>
> (1995: 3)

Morrison, Hong Kingston and Silko incorporate aspects of oral story-telling traditions, which are usually performed in interactive groups.

The storyteller, who can alter the story each time it is told can be asked questions by the listener who thereby guides the storyteller. This interactive storytelling is thought to promote communities by binding people together in a creative act. Moreover, because each time the story is told it is altered, it is understood that there is no one correct version of the story and that in fact, there are many. As Maggie Sale notes, in reference to Toni Morrison's adoption of African American 'call and response' storytelling techniques, 'This approach encourages multiple ways of seeing and interpreting, and so gives readers access to difficult material that encourages responses that are . . . complex and contradictory' (1992: 44). The adaptation of oral storytelling techniques in a magical realist narrative are complementary and mutually supportive. In a text where categories between the real and the magical have already been broken down, allowing for more than one version of truth to be proposed, the use of such storytelling techniques which assume that there are multiple versions of a story, emphasizes the possibility of expressing multiple perspectives in the text. As Zamora and Faris point out, this creates the radical position that magical realism 'resists the basic assumptions of post-enlightenment rationalism and literary realism' (1995: 6).

ONTOLOGICAL MAGICAL REALISM

Since he first presented his ideas on Latin American marvellous realism in 1949, Alejo Carpentier reiterated them, even as late at 1975, stating that 'our own marvelous real is encountered in its raw state, latent and omnipresent, in all that is Latin American. Here the strange is commonplace, and always was commonplace' (1995b: 104). Carpentier claimed that his version of magical realism, 'the marvellous real', found a natural home in Latin America. This he argued was in opposition to European magic realism, which he criticized for developing magic(al) realist techniques simply for narrative effect and without any connection to the cultural context in which it was produced. Carpentier saw the multiethnic and multicultural mix of Latin America and the cultural practices such as voodoo that resulted from it, as providing the perfect raw materials for a sense of the magical real in everyday life. He even provided a historical context for the development of Latin American magical realism, referring back to Hernando Cortés' impression that the experiences of Latin America from a European perspective were beyond words.

These ideas have instigated a debate amongst critics of magical realist fiction. Some, such as Amaryll Chanady, criticize Carpentier for attempting to appropriate a narrative mode (that she claims cannot be specific to any one culture) in order to boost the status of a geographical location's literary tradition – that of Latin America (1985: 131). Other contemporary critics, such as Roberto González Echevarría, have attempted to expand on Carpentier's suggestion that magical realist ideas can originate from a particular cultural context where they are compatible with the belief systems of that culture, although, like Chanady, they do not associate magical realism with just one culture such as that of Latin America. In a study of the work of Carpentier written in 1974, Echevarría distinguishes two forms of magical realism: the ontological and the epistemological. Ontological magical realism can be described as magical realism that has as its source material beliefs or practices from the cultural context in which the text is set. For instance, Carpentier's *The Kingdom of this World* includes a character called Mackandal who has the ability to change shape at will and even to take animal form. Mackandal is in fact a historical figure who led the slave uprising on Haiti and upon whom the novel is based. As Carpentier states, 'Yet in America . . . Mackandal lived and was endowed with the same powers by the faith of his contemporaries who with this magic fomented one of the strangest and most dramatic uprisings in history' (1995a: 87). He was thought to have magical powers such as the example of shape-shifting that Carpentier adopts for his novel and is a reference to the Haitian belief in man's ability to change shape at will and to take the form of an animal. This is a recognized aspect of Caribbean mythology which recurs in books such as Pauline Melville's collection of short stories entitled *Shape-Shifter* (1990), and is a trace of West African culture retained by the slave population.

Epistemological magical realism, on the other hand, takes its inspiration for its magical realist elements from sources which do not necessarily coincide with the cultural context of the fiction, or for that matter, of the writer. Jeanne Delbaere identified a similar difference between what she called folkloric magic realism (similar to the ontological) and scholarly magic realism (similar to the epistemological) in which the magical realism originates either from a particular folk tradition, or is cultivated from a variety of traditions in order to produce a particular narrative effect (1992: 76). The work of the Flemish writer Hubert Lampo is a good example of such epistemological magical realism, as he acknowledges that he was interested in using magical realist techniques in order to express the mood of Belgium but also to be a part of a larger international literary movement (1993: 33). He draws his magical realist aspects from many sources, but particularly from Greek and Roman mythology. While there is an argument that Greek and Roman mythology have influenced Western European culture, its influence is so historically and geographically removed that this argument does not convince sufficiently to support a claim that Lampo's magical realism originates predominantly in Flemish folklore with its Germanic roots.

There are problems with the assumptions that these terms carry which we must consider before continuing further. First, the division of magical realist writing into the categories of epistemological and ontological gives rise to the inappropriate suggestion that a writer can only create one or the other. In particular, this gives the misleading impression that a writer of ontological magical realism is debarred from using the narrative mode for reasons of literary experimentation or for intellectual reasons. It gives the impression, in other words, that ontological magical realist writers produce magical realist fiction because that is what they automatically write, and that they cannot take a distanced intellectual view of their writing. Gabriel García Márquez is a perfect example of why such an assumption is wrong. Whilst talking about his work he has taken the ontological position, emphasizing his belief in Latin American mythology; 'I am a realist writer . . . because I believe that in Latin American everything is possible, everything is real' (García Márquez and Vargas Llosa 1967: 19), whilst also expressing the epistemological position that is led by his knowledge and understanding of literature; 'I believe that what we should do is to promote it as a term of reality which can give something new to universal literature' (Irish 1974: no ref).

However, if we are to identify those writers whose magical realism originates predominantly from the beliefs of their own cultural context, we find that ontological magical realism, in fact, has become the most common and most recognized form of magical realism. Writers such as García Márquez, Rushdie, Morrison and Okri all derive the magical realist elements of their texts from the mythology, cultural beliefs and folklore of the cultural context in which their fiction is set – which is also their own. García Márquez has often noted that his magical realism comes from his grandmother's method of storytelling, and her stories that included folktales and superstitions from their rural region of Colombia (Williams 1985: 6). As an example, he cites the superstition that an incestuous relationship will result in the birth of children with pigs' tails. He incorporates this superstition into his novel *One Hundred Years of Solitude* when Ursula is gripped with fear of the consequence of her incestuous relationship with her husband, and the superstition eventually comes true when the third child, Aureliano, is born with a tail. Rushdie calls García Márquez's source of magical realism a 'village world-view', meaning that it is the result of a belief system developed in a rural environment and Rushdie implies that this is one that is little affected by modern scientific explanation (1991: 301). It is the importance of García Márquez as a magical realist that has led his folkloric Latin American 'village world-view' to be associated with magical realism as a narrative mode. This has caused writers such as Toni Morrison to dismiss the claim that she is a magical realist because, as she states, it appears that she is copying Latin American culture and doesn't have 'a culture to write out of . . . ' (Gilroy 1993: 181). However, writers such as Morrison base their magical realism in the belief systems of their own cultural group rather than that of a particular location such as Latin America. Her locations vary between city, suburb, town and countryside but her magical realism is inspired by the residual influence of the belief systems of the African American slaves of the eighteenth and nineteenth centuries. These slaves, having been brought predominantly from West Africa, were forced to lose their language and beliefs and to adopt the English language and Christianity. Particularly during the second half of the twentieth century, critics such as Henry Louis Gates have retraced many cultural aspects common to African Americans to the cultures of West Africa. These include lines and stories from spirituals, folktales and the patterns of music, speech and storytelling. With this knowledge, Morrison's fiction attempts to recreate a communal history for African Americans which links them back to the painful past of slavery and what was done to them and she emphasizes the cultural traits that link them to that history. Her magical realism includes characters who can fly back to Africa when they die. This was a commonly known myth amongst African American slaves.

As it is a recovered myth, Morrison herself is unsure of her own absolute belief in the flying slaves but is convinced by the cultural importance of such a myth. She claims that her novel *The Song of Solomon*:

> is about Black people who could fly. That was always part of the folklore of my life; flying was one of our gifts. I don't care how silly it may seem . . . It is everywhere . . . people used to talk about it, it's in the spirituals and gospels. Perhaps it was wishful thinking . . . But suppose it wasn't?
>
> (LeClair 1994: 122)

The importance for Morrison of referring to these African American myths is that they rekindle the connections to their own distinct culture; one that developed through adaptation to their circumstances in America but which retained certain similar cultural traits to West Africa and which was brutally suppressed by slave owners and by the continuation of racist segregation laws into the twentieth century.

The West African writer Ben Okri uses the Yoruba myths and belief systems from Nigeria to illustrate the effects of colonialism. His novel *The Famished Road*, in particular, is built around the Yoruba notion of the simultaneous coexistence and connections between the worlds of the living and the dead. According to Brenda Cooper the appearance of the dead in the realm of the living is a negative 'commentary on the health of the human condition' (1998: 50). In the setting of the novel, the poor state of the human condition reflects the disastrous consequences of colonization and of the corruption of post-independence politicians in Nigeria.

What is also remarkable about the use of magical realism by these writers is that they employ the mode not only because they wish to repeat folkloric mythologies from their cultural community, but because they wish to promote a greater depth of understanding of the present circumstances in which the texts were written. For instance, García Márquez has claimed that he wants to bring back the imaginary into Latin American culture but also to write fiction that counters its destructive present-day atmosphere of political corruption. As Rushdie comments:

> The damage to reality in South America is at least as much political as cultural. In García Márquez's experience, truth has been controlled to

> the point at which it has ceased to be possible to find out what it is. The
> only truth is that you are being lied to all the time.
>
> (1991: 301).

Morrison has said that she wishes to make her fiction useful for present day African Americans in order for them to be able to move on from the past of slavery. Rushdie's novels provide commentary on the dangers and pitfalls of contemporary cultural politics and attitudes in India and Britain.

One question in relation to the concept of ontological magical realism remains unanswered and that is whether magical realism can be ontological when its sources are drawn from the context in which the novel is set but where these do not coincide with the culture of the writer. For instance, Alejo Carpentier, although from the culturally mixed region of the Caribbean, was a Cuban of European origin who spent much time living in Europe, where in fact he was introduced to the idea of magic realism. To what extent can he be said to share the cultural context of Haitian slaves with West African cultural influences from previous centuries? This question will remain unanswered in this section but it is a line of enquiry which will be considered again in relation to the future of magical realism in the final chapter. It is this form of questioning concerning the cultural position of the magical realist writer and critic that is most commonly posed.

POSTCOLONIAL MAGICAL REALISM

The majority of magical realist writing can be described as postcolonial. That is to say much of it is set in a postcolonial context and written from a postcolonial perspective that challenges the assumptions of an authoritative colonialist attitude. As we can see from our discussions of transgressive, crosscultural and postmodern magical realism, these variants seek to disrupt official and defined authoritative assumptions about reality, truth and history. In particular the proliferation of magical realist writing in English in the closing decades of the twentieth century has coincided with the rise of the postcolonial novel to such an extent that postcolonial critics such as Elleke Boehmer in her guide to colonial and postcolonial literature see the two as 'almost inextricable' (1995: 235).

Postcolonialism, like postmodernism, is a complex term that is still being debated and transformed. Essentially it refers to the political and social attitude that opposes colonial power, recognizes the effects of colonialism on other nations, and refers specifically to nations which have gained independence from the rule of another imperial state. Postcolonial writing can be, as in the writing of Robert Kroetsch in 1970s' Canada, a way of reconsidering the identity of a nation after independence or it can be a means of expressing opposition to the ideas of colonialism, such as in the work of Chinua Achebe in 1950s' and 1960s' Nigeria. It is generally agreed in postcolonial theory and criticism that the effects of colonialism were not just the imposition of one nation's rule over another, but it included attempts to change the colonized people's ways of thinking and belief to accept the cultural attitudes and definitions of the colonial power. This often involved the attempt by colonial rulers to define the colonized people and their nation from the colonizers' perspective and to impose a homogeneous, authoritative historical and cultural identity on the colonized nation. These disruptive and displacing effects on the cultural life of the colonized nation have been the most difficult aspects of colonialism to change. In his guide to postcolonialism, John McLeod is keen to emphasize the double faceted nature of this socio-political approach:

> 'postcolonialism' recognises both historical *continuity* and *change*. On the one hand, it acknowledges that the material realities and modes of representation common to colonialism are still very much with us today, even if the political map of the world has changed through decolonisation. But on the other hand, it asserts the promise, the possibility, and the continuing necessity to change, while also recognising that important challenges and changes have already been achieved.
>
> (2000: 33)

The majority of postcolonial theory and criticism, particularly that relating to literature, recognizes colonialism and postcolonialism as also a form of discourse, that is a socially and politically determined form of language and expression. Thus, postcolonial novels that are written in postcolonial discourse adopt assumptions and attitudes which are associated with a political perspective that opposes or recognizes the effects of colonialism on the context of the novel. For this reason, while many writers may not directly address the issue of colonialism or postcolonialism, their writing and the assumptions behind what they express reveal a concern with such political issues.

Summarizing her view of the closeness of magical realism to postcolonialism, Elleke Boehmer claims that:

> Drawing on the special effects of magic realism, postcolonial writers in English are able to express their view of a world fissured, distorted, and made incredible by cultural displacement . . . [T]hey combine the supernatural with local legend and imagery derived from colonialist cultures to represent societies which have been repeatedly unsettled by invasion, occupation, and political corruption. Magic effects, therefore, are used to indict the follies of both empire and its aftermath.
>
> (1995: 235)

There has been much discussion about how and why magical realist narratives are so suited to expressing postcolonial issues such as cultural distortion and displacement. The most often cited discussion is the 1988 theory of postcolonial magical realism proposed by the Canadian postmodernist critic Stephen Slemon. Although Slemon uses the term 'magic realism', his discussion refers to texts and characteristics that are commonly and more accurately identified as 'magical realism'. Calling on a mixture of postmodernist assumptions and the discourse theories of Mikhail Bakhtin, he claims that magical realism is able to express three postcolonial elements. First, due to its dual narrative structure, magical realism is able to present the postcolonial context from both the colonized peoples' and the colonizers' perspectives through its narrative structure as well as its themes. Second, it is able to produce a text which reveals the tensions and gaps of representation in such a context. Third, it provides a means to fill in the gaps of cultural representation in a postcolonial context by recuperating the fragments and voices of forgotten or subsumed histories from the point of view of the colonized.

Slemon adapts and simplifies Bakhtin's model of dialogic discourse to explain how the system of narrative tension works in a magical realist text. He explains that there are two discourses in the narrative but each with a different perspective, the magical and the real, and that neither is dominant but is in constant tension with and opposition to the other. As he explains, there are 'two opposing discursive systems, with neither managing to subordinate or contain the other' (1995: 410). As he sees it, this structure reflects the tension between the ever-present and ever-opposed colonized and colonialist discourses in a postcolonial context in which the narrative structure reflects the relationship between the two, so that the 'texts recapitulate a postcolonial account of the social and historical relations of the culture in which they are set' (1995: 409). In addition, the tension between the two systems means that there are 'gaps' in the narrative which can be read either as a negative gap that reflects the difficulty of cultural expression for the colonized in the oppositional face of the colonialist power, or it can provide a positive gap which can be filled with the expression of an alternative perspective from the colonized point of view. Slemon explains that this comes about because:

> a battle between two oppositional systems takes place, each working toward the creation of a different kind of fictional world from the other. Since the ground rules of these two worlds are incompatible, neither one can fully come into being, and each remains suspended, locked in a continuous disjunction within each of the separate discursive systems, rending them with gaps, absences and silences.
>
> (1995: 409)

Slemon refers to the Canadian writers Jack Hodgins and Robert Kroetsch to illustrate his theory. Here he deals with writers from what is known as a 'settler' postcolonial nation. Canada was settled by immigrants who originated from Britain, the imperialist power, and from other European nations. The settlers became the predominant population, dominating the indigenous population. This is in contrast to other postcolonial nations where the indigenous population remained in the majority and altered little in its composition during colonialism. These two forms of colonialism have been recognized by postcolonial critics to have different relationships with colonial power. However, Slemon uses these Canadian 'settler' postcolonial writers to illustrate the postcolonial condition in general. His analysis, therefore, needs to be read with that in mind. He chose these writers not only because as a critic he is predominantly concerned with Canadian postcolonialism but also because both writers are concerned with the effects of colonialism on identity. Hodgin's novel *The Invention of the World* follows the story of a community built as a replica of colonialism on Vancouver Island. Kroetsch's novel *What the Crow Said* describes the life of a small rural community on the borders of Saskatchewan and Alberta building a sense of who they are through the stories. Both writers attempt in their writing to create other ways of considering Canada as a postcolonial nation without having to rely on the image of Canada as defined by British imperialism. In order to do this, both writers use fragments of forgotten stories and orally transmitted tales to build an alternative history with which to consider Canadianness. As Slemon notes, these novels assume that colonialism has distorted their sense of identity and their relationship to their history. This occurs due to the Empire's power to define the history of its colonies to suit its own purposes. Slemon explains that colonialism is 'a condition of being both tyrannized by history and yet paradoxically cut off from it' (1995: 418). To move on from the colonized position, many writers such as Kroetsch and Hodgins attempt to reconstruct history from the remains of what is known of the people's history from their own perspective. As Slemon states, 'This imaginative reconstruction has echoes in those forms of postcolonial thought which seek to recuperate the lost voices and discarded fragments, that imperialist cognitive structures push to the margins of critical consciousness' (1995: 415). This means that many postcolonial texts (such as those by Toni Morrison that attempt to provide an alternative history to that supported by the dominant power) use oral storytelling as a source of alternative perspectives on history, as the oral tale was often the only way in which alternative versions of events that did not agree with those written as authoritative history survived. As Slemon points out, the political objective of these texts is that 'the dispossessed, the silenced, and the marginalized of our own dominating systems can again find voice' (1995: 422).

The South African writer André Brink provides an interesting example of a postcolonial settler writer whose work is predominantly concerned with the reconsideration and revision of history. Brink's magical realist novels including *The Devil's Valley* ([1999] 2000b) and

Imaginings of Sand ([1996] 2000a) are written from the postcolonial, post-apartheid, dispossessed perspective of an Afrikaner male. Although having been subject to imposed British colonial rule since the middle of the nineteenth century, this minority community still maintained a dominant position over the indigenous population until the fall of apartheid. Having lost their dominance, Brink explores the desperation and loss of identity through the eyes of a disenchanted urban and educated Afrikaner. His novel *The Devil's Valley* reveals a grotesque community in which any involvement with the indigenous population was punishable by death; any reference even to the punishments was taboo, despite the fact that the narrator is able to trace communal myths and beliefs to the local indigenous community. The magical aspects of the novel include the appearance of the dead founder of the community amongst the living, the ethereal nature of one of the girls who leaves no footprints, and the strange nocturnal activities of the girls of the community who seem to be a group of witches. Rather than providing light relief, these magical aspects are highly disturbing for the narrator protagonist, Flip Lochner, who attempts to record an authoritative history of the community. The South African critic Marita Wenzel in an essay on Brink's magical realism notes that the novel reveals its attitudes to history, and concludes that reality, absolute truth and history are unknowable. Indeed, all of the attempts made by Flip Lochner to record an authoritative history are disrupted either by losing his camera and tape recorder, or by the conflicting stories that he is told by different members of the community. He eventually notes that he will not be able to create one version of the history of the community, not only because so many aspects are hidden from him, but also because 'I suspect that even if I were to know all there would still not be a whole, just an endless gliding from one to another' (Brink 2000b: 368). Lochner eventually settles on gaining an understanding of the community through its diversity and the multiple perspectives which constitute it, rather than attempting to recreate a homogeneous authoritative history. In other words, Brink's protagonist settles for a postcolonial historical perspective from the point of view of all the people involved, rather than seeking to impose his authoritative view of how he interprets their history in the manner of a colonialist. This denouement to Brink's novel is perfectly illustrative of the critic Marie Vautier's summary of the power of magical realist postcolonial novels:

'Magic realist works, however, bear witness to their liberation from a teleological and homogeneous historical discourse and to an acceptance of postcolonial heterogeneity with regard to historiography and to myth' (1998: 205).

The critic Michael Dash carried out a study of marvellous realism in the Caribbean in 1974, in which he too noted the close relationship of history to postcolonialism for non-settler, post-slavery nations. In a comparison of writers of the '*négritude*' movement of the 1930s which sought to connect the people of the Caribbean with their slave ancestors and African culture and history, Dash notes that what is referred to as magical realism provides a means to recover not only the past but also the creative and spiritual aspects of the colonized people. He notes that these writers 'have turned to the myths, legends and superstitions of the folk in order to isolate traces of a complex culture of survival which was the response of the dominated to their oppressors' (Dash 1974: 66). Focusing his analysis on the writing of British Guyanese Wilson Harris (1921–), he notes that such writing, like that of Alejo Carpentier ten years before, draws on voodoo and Amerindian culture for inspiration to recreate a spriritual and mythical cultural resource for the people of this ex-British colony. Harris himself is very aware of the postcolonial need for such recuperation, and is quoted by Dash as saying 'the imagination of the fold involved a crucial inner re-creative response to the violations of slavery and indenture and conquest' (1974: 66). To summarize, Dash claims that such marvellous realist writing of the middle to late twentieth-century Caribbean is:

> the taking into account of the inner resources that the ancestors of the Third World could have developed to combat their tragic environment, therefore engaging in a conception of the past which would shatter the myth of 'historylessness' or 'non-achievement'.
>
> (1974: 66)

This appears to be what García Márquez attempts to do with his stories of the fictional isolated and unsophisticated town of Macondo. The population of Macondo are only considered to be important for a short period of history by the banana plantation owners, but generally the township is outside of history, marginalized from modernity and power.

It is only through the visits of the gypsies that the people of Macondo become aware of scientific discoveries. However, the attraction of writing about such a place for García Márquez is to emphasize the richness of their cultural and mythic life, and the importance of a pluralist story-telling rather than authoritative historical narrative. The critic Kum Kum Sangari wrote an essay in 1987 in which she considered the postcolonial aspects of what she called the marvellous realism of both García Márquez and Rushdie. Although Latin American writers are often not discussed in postcolonial criticism, Sangari puts forward a convincing argument for considering García Márquez in these terms. She explains that, for her:

> Marvellous realism answers an emergent society's need for renewed self-description, and radical assessment, displaces the established categories through which the West had construed other cultures either in its own image or as alterity, questions the western capitalist myth of modernization and progress, and asserts without nostalgia an indigenous preindustrial realm of possibility.
>
> (Sangari 1987: 162)

This chapter has demonstrated that magical realism provides a means for writers to express a non-dominant or non-Western perspective, whether that be from a feminist, postcolonial or rural standpoint, in opposition to dominant cultural discourse. It can be, in its transgressive, subversive and revisionary aspects, a revolutionary form of writing. The final chapter will explore the way in which the association of magical realism with non-Western cultures can equally provide a politically ambiguous situation in which the very magical realism itself seems to emphasize a Western perspective despite its attempts to portray a non-Western one. As Brenda Cooper explains, 'magical realism and its associated styles and devices is alternatively characterized as a transgressive mechanism that parodies Authority, the Establishment and the Law, and also as the opposite of all of these, as a domain of play, desire and fantasy for the rich and powerful' (1998: 29).

6

MAGIC(AL) REALISM AND CULTURAL PRODUCTION

Up to this point the focus of this book has been on magical realism in adult narrative fiction. However, this chapter, which considers magic(al) realist cultural production discusses magical realism and magic realism where they appear in other cultural forms such as television, film and painting. It opens with a discussion of the appearance of magical realism in children's literature in English such as that by Edith Nesbit and Michael Bond, then children's television and particularly narrative drama. The section also considers the role of magical realism in film as a narrative art form. In order to do this, films such as Wim Wenders' *Wings of Desire* are considered in the light of the way in which the narrative of the film is told, whether through dialogue or filming techniques. Film has been considered in magic realist terms by a few critics such as Fredric Jameson, but for the most part, many magical realist films have not been analysed from this point of view, unless adapted from a recognized magical realist novel, such as *Como agua para chocolate* (*Like Water for Chocolate*). Finally, this chapter will consider magic realism in painting. As the term 'magic realism' was coined in relation to a particular form of painting, there is much critical work exploring these paintings in such terms. The sections analysing painting will identify the main practitioners of this form, such as Otto Dix, Georg Schrimpf, Alex Colville and Frida Kahlo, and will demonstrate how it has remained a current critical form in art.

MAGICAL REALISM AND CHILDREN'S CULTURE

There is much in children's culture, that is, in cultural items produced for children, that can be associated with magical realism. Much recent children's culture, particularly literature and television for children in the English language, has adopted magical realism. Although fairy tales are not 'magical realist', since the stories takes place on another plane of reality from our own, we, as children, grow accustomed to understanding that these narratives can be related to our own reality at some interpretative level. I want to argue that magical realism provides a perfect means for children to explore the world through their imaginations without losing a connection to what they recognize as the 'real world'. Children's literature critic Roger Drury explains that 'a child seems positively obsessed by a need to experiment with ways of looking at the world, to rearranging place and time, to challenge the stable and predictable frame of experience' (1977: 180). Moreover, critic Peter Hunt suggests that young children often prefer texts to resolve unusual situations and restore normality (1991: 127). Because of this, many magical happenings in children's fiction occur in ordinary settings for limited periods of time while maintaining a close connection with reality. Magical realist children's fiction offers the opportunity for children to explore disruptions in their ordinary world secure in the knowledge that such magic and extraordinariness can be contained.

In her 1988 study of magic in children's literature, Maria Nikolajeva follows the development of children's literature from dream fantasies that include other worlds, to modern family stories that deploy incidental magic. According to Nikolajeva, the inclusion of magic in children's literature, rather than fairy tale, developed only after the influence of German romanticism in the late nineteenth century, which brought with it an interest in folk tradition (1988: 14).

In English, the writer that first approached the idea of magical realism was the trail-blazing late-Victorian English children's writer Edith Nesbit (1858–1924). Nesbit wrote books which later became known as 'modern fantasy' and which were revolutionary in that they rejected the adult moral tone used by so many children's writers before her. As Nikolajeva explains:

> she flatly rejected Victorian didacticism with its manner of talking down to children. She started using the real, spoken language which makes her books readable today. She portrayed real, human, blood-and-flesh characters instead of the earlier absolutely virtuous, angelic children.

(1988: 16)

By using the language of children and basing her characters' actions on the behaviour of actual children she approached a much more realist form of children's literature. This provided a realistic base for her occasional magic which occurs in the lives of her child characters, and opens the possibility for us to examine her work as magical realist. Two of her earlier novels, *Five Children and It* ([1902] 1979) and *The Phoenix and the Carpet* ([1904] 1979) provide good examples of how Nesbit's writing approaches the model of magical realism. Both stories follow events in the lives of a family of children who are left alone for long periods of time. Their parents or nanny only appear momentarily to say goodnight or to carry out a household chore. The children are naturally inquisitive and this leads them to discover, first, a sand fairy called 'It' on their holiday beach and later a phoenix in their fire grate which arrived with their new (magical) carpet. Although the magical figures It and the phoenix are extraordinary characters, both have an extremely good command of English and see themselves as adamantly ordinary figures who communicate easily with the children. Once the sand fairy is found, he is insulted that the children do not recognize him. He tells them "'Upon my word! Why, you talk as if I were nobody in particular!" All its fur stood out like a cat's when it is going to fight' (Nesbit 1979: 21). His indignation adds to the magical realist assumption that even if the children (and the reader) do not know what a sand fairy is, it is their lack of knowledge not his extraordinariness that is at fault. The phoenix is also an enigma to the children who are only able to identify him by using a reference book. The magical realist appearance of the phoenix is typical of Nesbit's 'modern fantasy' and emphasizes the immediate relationship between the children and the extraordinary creature. The phoenix does not introduce himself to the children but talks to them as though he already knew them. The children's reaction is equally fitting with magical realism: 'They were not astonished but they were very, very interested' (Nesbit 1979: 198). In fact, *The Phoenix and the Carpet* has elements which are similar to the magical realism of García Márquez (writing over fifty years later). For instance, the phoenix creates a distortion in the concept of time by ageing more rapidly than humans. As he explains, '"Time . . . is as you are probably aware, merely a convenient fiction. There is no such thing as time. I have lived in two months at a pace which generously counterbalanced five hundred years of life in the desert"' (Nesbit 1979: 369). In addition, where magical realism assumes that the magical elements have a logic of their own, Nesbit also insisted that the magic in her stories had rules. Nikolajeva notes that, 'Magic in Nesbit's books is so logical and consequent that it does not need explanation' (1988: 28).

However, the work of Nesbit differs significantly from magical realism in one aspect. Nesbit was very clear in her commentary on her writing, and her narratorial interventions in the stories themselves, that adults are restricted from recognizing the ordinary nature of magic. In the opening chapter of *Five Children and It* she explains to the assumed child reader:

> you may leave the book about quite safely, for no adults and uncles are likely to write 'How true!' on the edge of the story. Grown up people find it very difficult to believe really wonderful things, unless they have what they call proof.
>
> (Nesbit 1979: 16)

Little did she guess of the reading habits of us magical realists to come . . . ! In *The Phoenix and the Carpet*, the adults are actually oblivious to any magical changes that occur for their children. The narrator comments on this and creates the access to magic, or lack of it, as a defining feature separating childhood from adulthood; 'Father and mother had not the least idea of what had happened in their absence. This is often the case, even when there are no magic carpets or Phoenixes in the house' (Nesbit 1979: 205). Indeed, Nikolejeva's assessment of Nesbit's influence on twentieth-century children's literature in English emphasizes those aspects which we consider to be magical realist. She notes:

> This clash of the magical and the ordinary, the unexpected conse-quences of magic when introduced in the everyday realistic life is the cornerstone of Nesbit's fantasy. This is the principally new feature which has become the key notion of the twentieth century fantasy, of what may be called "modern fantasy".
>
> (Nikolejeva 1988: 16)

In the mid-twentieth century, the preferred format of modern children's fantasy in both the United States and Britain was to take Nesbit's model of the story of the ordinary family and introduce an animal with human behaviour. In both the stories of *A Bear Called Paddington* ([1958] 2001) by Michael Bond in the United Kingdom, and *Stuart Little* ([1945] 1969) by E. B. White in the United States, animals with the characteristics of a human child, and most particularly innocence, are either born into a human family (the mouse, Stuart Little) or are adopted by them (Paddington). For Louisa Smith this form of story is a vehicle for moral teaching because of the close relationship between the elements of fantasy and recognizable reality (1996: 296). The observations of the narratives enable distinctions to be made between what is acceptable behaviour and what is inappropriate behaviour in the context of a family and of society.

The logic of such stories revolves around what is the ordinariness of the animal character in the eyes of the narrator, reader and the family, but what is extraordinariness in the eyes of the peripheral characters. For instance, Paddington Bear is introduced to the reader with the following lines, 'Mr and Mrs Brown first met Paddington on a railway platform. In fact, that was how he came to have such an unusual name for a bear' (Bond 2001: 7). The extraordinary element of this passage is not that a bear may have a name, or that he may be in a railway station in central London, but that his name is unusual. This places the reader in the position of being in collusion with the narrator, resulting in the acceptance of the different rules governing 'normal behaviour' in the unusual context of the story. Such animal stories rely on a delicate balance between humour deriving from unusual behaviour and maintaining ordinariness. For instance, when Paddington is taken to a café, he draws the disapproving attention of the other customers. The narrative reports that this is because he creates a mess while eating, rather than, as we might expect, because he is extraordinary.

In a move away from Nesbit's model, many mid- and late twentieth-century stories include adult characters in the magical happenings. The story of *Bednob and Broomstick* ([1947] 1970) by Mary Norton includes adults with magical talents who bring escapism from the tedium of real life and kindness to the neglected child characters. The children left in the care of their uninterested relatives in *Bednob and Broomstick* receive kind attention and a flying bed from the trainee witch Miss Price. In children's fiction these adults are often notable for their innocence in contrast to the other adults around them and provide hope and an increased sense of security in relation to the adult world the children know that they must enter one day.

Influenced by such children's literature, there has been a growing trend in magical realist television dramas and films for children after the 1970s. Beginning with the British Broadcasting Corporation adaptations for television of Nesbit's novels, and a cartoon version of the Paddington Bear stories, many dramas written for children's television have followed the magical realist mode. Increasingly sophisticated film technology means that the non-human characters or magical happenings can be presented with more seamless realism than before. A film of *Stuart Little* directed by Robert Minkoff in 1999 uses computer animation techniques in order to fit the mouse-like figure of Stuart into the scenes with human actors and real-life settings.

One of the most popular children's stories of recent years, *Matilda* by Roald Dahl ([1988] 2001), provides the model for a new direction for domestic fantasy. It is the child protagonist Matilda who has magical powers and is able to transform her life and those around her. In previously written domestic fantasy, such as the stories of Mary Norton and E. Nesbit, it is more usual for magic to be brought to the children by another being or person who helps them combat the negative aspects of their lives. Dahl empowers his child character Matilda who is able to challenge by means of magic and defeat the most tyrannical of adults such as the immense ex-hammer-throwing, bullying schoolmistress Miss Trunchbull. Although the setting of J. K. Rowling's Harry Potter stories in the parallel world of Hogwarts School diminishes their likeness to magical realism, they too reveal empowered children transforming the adult world with their own magical powers.

We can conclude that children have access to many stories which prepare them to accept magical realist fiction as adults. These stories often provide moral teaching or social critique in an entertaining form much as adult magical realism often provides commentary on real political situations. While domestic fantasy and magical children's fiction does not follow every defining element of magical realism, they provide an interesting insight into assumptions about the relationship of magic to everyday reality, and the human need to learn this process at an early age. Perhaps we should question the extent to which readers of magical realism are simply reluctant to give up their childhood approach to stories.

MAGIC(AL) REALISM IN FILM

Film is not often considered as magic(al) realist in criticism and neither magic realism nor magical realism are recognized categories of film. However, it is possible to recognize features of both magic realism and magical realism in many films. Like Fredric Jameson, you can take a critical approach that explores the images of film using the same skills employed by visual art critics. His essay 'On Magic Realism in Film', written in 1986, is the only essay to explore the genre of film as magic realism. He analyses several Latin American films produced during the 1980s which use the same cold, detailed, close focus approach of magic realist painting as outlined by Franz Roh, to portray the shocking reality of gratuitous violence. This approach is difficult to detect in film where, for instance, the photographic smooth surface of the painting studied by Roh is the norm in cinema, and grainy film techniques are less common. Where grainy film texture is visible it is not necessarily indicative of an artistic approach because, as Jameson points out, film texture is sometimes beyond the control of the director due to a lack of funds to buy smooth high quality film (1986: 316). Close-ups on objects, which might indicate a magic realist interest in the qualities of the object (the increased objectivity), might simply be a part of a montage of shots combined to create the story. Alternatively, it is possible to analyse films as magical realist narratives, as stories told through the medium of film, using similar skills as those used to analyse literature. As the film critic Tom Gunning points out, if film is considered to be a narrative art form it is one of the most directly realistic, as there is often no apparent narrator and the action and the actors appear to be real, actual and present: 'its inherent photographic tendency towards mimesis, toward the representation of a world from which the filmic narrator can seem to be absent' (1999: 465).

The analysis of film adaptations of magical realist novels from the page to the screen provides a means to consider how the visual elements affect the narrative magical realism. There are several well-known film adaptations of magical realist novels worth considering such as the adaptation by Alfonso Arau in 1992 of Laura Esquivel's novel *Como agua para chocolate* (*Like Water for Chocolate*). The film adaptation of *Like Water for Chocolate* retains the key magical realist events in the novel that occur due to the transmission of emotion through food. The wedding of Pedro to his lover Tita's sister ends with the guests being overcome by the nausea of sadness first felt by Tita during her making of the wedding cake. The transmission of Tita's passion for Pedro through a dish of partridges and rose petals leads to the elopement of her sister Gertrudis with a passing soldier which is a consequence of her literally burning with passion. The episode when Gertrudis burns down the shower house with her body-heat is easily illustrated in the film. Gertrudis' rising passion is shown by the stereotypical action of running of her hands over her body and with steam and flames rising from the floor as she showers. Despite the increased sense of reality for the viewer as they witness actually enacted events unfold on the screen, the realism of the film is diminished by the director's choice of lighting. The film is almost entirely shot with a golden light and contrasting deep shade. This provides a romantic atmosphere for the film and diminishes the sense of everyday reality, and is far removed from the clarity of light identified by Franz Roh in magic realist painting. This film is an emotional film above all. It is filmed in close-up so that emotional reactions to the events registered on the character's faces become the focus of the viewer's attention. Whilst this in itself does not diminish the realism found in the novel, it diverts the viewer's attention away from the horror of the rape and murder of the women of the household by bandits. Unlike those films referred to by Jameson, in this film the violence occurs off screen. In addition, the film includes the story of the civil war soldiers, but not to engineer a contrast between the realism of the violence of the era and the domestic lives of the women in the house, but rather for comic relief. One soldier, Treviño, is the fool of the film who has to be dragged away from the women he adores. In the book, Treviño is popular with the women servants, but he is also a ruthlessly violent killer.

Among the many films which have magical realist events or elements there are few which maintain as consistent a magical realist narrative perspective as the 1987 film *Der Himmel über Berlin* (literally translated as 'Heaven Over Berlin' but titled in English *Wings of Desire*) by the German director Wim Wenders. The film, based on the novel by Peter Handke, follows the lives of two angels who live over Berlin and act as witnesses to the inner lives of the people of the city. The film depicts the collision of two different and coexisting worlds, that of the angels and of the humans, when one of the angels, Damiel, chooses to become human. The contrasting mixture of the realism of Berlin life and the magical appearance of angels produces an unarguably magical realist setting and narrative. The film explores the paradoxical situation of the angels who are able to observe intimately the emotional lives of the residents of Berlin, but who cannot participate in or experience any physical aspect of life. As with many magical realist novels, the narrative technique of the film and the content are intertwined. The narrative perspective is indicated by the use of colour on the screen. When the narrative perspective is that of the angels the film is shot in black and white, whereas when it is told from a human perspective it is in colour. The majority of the narrative is told from the perspectives of the angels and we, the viewers, are asked to identify ourselves with their position. However, towards the end the narrative perspective shifts to that of Damiel in human form experiencing sensual life for the first time. The film ends with the joyful scene in colour of the angel-come-human Damiel helping Marion to fly on her trapeze. To one side of the main scene, the angel Cassiel sits and watches surrounded by a halo of monochrome. In essence, this device appears to indicate, optimistically, that it is better to live the full experience and reality of life than to be protected magically from its traumas. Unusually for magical realist narratives, ultimately, the realist element is celebrated in contrast to the magical.

The magical realism of *Wings of Desire* is close to that of E. Nesbit's domestic fantasy. As in the stories of E. Nesbit, there are rules governing the magical appearance of the angels in Berlin. The angels are not visible to most people, and are only occasionally seen by children. They are not able to influence the lives of people but can provide comfort, and most importantly, they are not able to experience the human senses. However, this division breaks down when the angels meet a man who is able to sense them and talk to them with a depth of understanding of their situation. This man is the actual American actor Peter Falk filming a story about his most famous character, the detective Columbo from the American television series of the same name (1971–8). The appearance of Falk playing both himself in the film, and the fictional Columbo, makes the complexity of realism in film evident to the viewers, in that we are made aware that he is a real person but becomes another who is accepted as real when on film. To add to this complexity, it is implied in the film that Peter Falk is able to sense and discuss the materiality of life in contrast to the ethereality of angels because he was an angel who has become human. This plot device provides us with a typically double-edged magical realist situation. If Falk is real and he has been an angel then we can assume that angels are real. However, the fact that Falk is playing himself as an actor playing a character in a film disrupts the realism of the film. This aspect of the film indicates that it belongs to the postmodern era in which it was filmed. The lack of a certain answer concerning the nature of reality is in keeping with the critic Brian McHale's notion that postmodernism is ontological and concerns itself with questions of discontinuous being. He proposes that postmodernist works ask questions such as 'What kinds of worlds are there, how are they constituted, and how do they differ? What happens when different kinds of worlds are placed in confrontation, or when boundaries between worlds are violated?' (McHale 1987: 10).

In the 1997 realist full-colour remake of *Wings of Desire* under the title *City of Angels* directed by Brad Siberling the question of the existence of a spiritual life independent from bodily form is emphasized. The angel Seth falls in love with a young female surgeon, Maggie, who is having a crisis of confidence in her work leading her to question whether it is she, God or fate that decides the outcome of her operations. Although Seth eventually finds joy in experiencing the sensations of his own existence, the tragic climax, which occurs when Maggie is killed in a road accident after Seth has become human in order to live with her, leaves unanswered the questions Maggie poses.

This postmodern ambiguous attitude towards the existence of angels in the 1980s film *Wings of Desire* is in contrast to the seminal film concerning angels, *It's a Wonderful Life* (1946) by Frank Capra. This film can be described as magical realist in many of its scenes and is also a story that contains a guardian angel. Rather than being left with an ambiguous sense of reality as in *Wings of Desire*, the plot of *It's a Wonderful Life* leads the central character to a secure sense of his own reality which includes the total belief in the existence of angels. It is the story of an ordinary man 'George' who is struggling in a small town existence against rampant capitalism and the expectations of him as a son, husband and father. The film opens in the present narrative time to reveal the setting of the story in a recognizably realistic small, friendly town at Christmastime. This very real setting is placed in contrast to the next scene which consists of voices seemingly coming from three twinkling stars in the night sky. The stars, who are 'The Boss', Joseph and Clarence, discuss the predicament of George and it becomes apparent due to the reference to wings that they are angels. Although magical, the discussion of the angels is carried out in the highly realistic language and tone of a business meeting in which they prepare Clarence for his 'mission' to save George. In a stroke of film genius, Capra uses the fact that Joseph is an angel and can see all things at all times in order to narrate George's life. Through the use of his magical powers, Joseph shows Clarence a movie-like summary of George's life. Thus, the visual images shared by Joseph and Clarence also constitute the story presented on the screen. Through this device the viewer and Clarence witness George's life from his boyhood to the present narrative time to reveal that he has been brought to bankruptcy and is contemplating suicide. When Clarence saves George from drowning and reveals himself to him by the river, the full extent of the magical realism of the film becomes apparent. Clarence is matter-of-fact and almost flippant regarding his condition as an angel. He tells George in a matter-of-fact tone that he is an 'AS2 (Angel, second class)' and that in order to 'gain his wings' he needs to save George from despair and loss of faith. The film follows George's journey from loss of faith to belief and the acceptance of the existence of angels.

The fact that the protagonist of the film, George, initially, is doubtful about the existence of angels does not detract from the magical realism of the film since the point of view of the film is not that of George but of the angel Joseph. Therefore, when Clarence grants George's wish that he should never have been born and shows him his town and family under such circumstances, George's confusion does not create doubt for the viewer.

The film ends after Clarence has restored George's faith in the world and with it his belief in the existence of angels. In effect, the narrative is the recovery of a man losing his faith in the central pillars of American society: family, community and religion. The film presents itself as a moral tale to encourage the respect of such aspects of society. However, the final scene of the film not only concludes George's return to the centre of his family and community but also acts as a reconfirmation of the reality of the magical elements of the narrative. George finds a gift of a book by his Christmas tree from Clarence, proving beyond doubt to the viewer, the physical existence of Clarence.

In a different vein, magical realism comes close to science fiction in a film such as Spike Jonze's *Being John Malkovich* (1999). This film is set in a world recognizable to the viewer but with one unusual element. The protagonist of the film, a young clerk, finds himself working on 'the seventh-and-a-half floor', which has half the ceiling height of any other floor. The unusual quality of the floor is accepted without question by the other workers. Both the protagonist and the viewer also become accustomed to the unusual setting of the story and this prepares both to accept the absurd discovery of a magical portal behind a cupboard into the brain of the actor John Malkovich. This portal could be described as a 'novum' or fictional invention in the terms of science fiction but this does not detract from the magical realist element of the film. The magical realism of the film is made clear by the unsurprised acceptance of the magic by the majority of the characters. This is supported by highly realistic details of the set. Additionally, like Peter Falk in *Wings of Desire*, John Malkovich plays a fictional version of himself in this film. Paradoxically, Malkovich's appearance as a character based closely on his real life self emphasizes the realism of the film but also adds to the viewer's awareness of the fictional nature of what they are viewing. Malkovich, after all, has to act not only as himself but also someone whose thoughts are being taken over by another.

The common aspect of all of these films, but most particularly of *Wings of Desire*, *City of Angels* and *Being John Malkovich*, is that the magical realist element of the film acts as a means of initiating questions concerning philosophical issues such as the existence of God, the role of fate, and the idea of the self that extend beyond the film's capacity to divert and entertain.

MAGIC(AL) REALIST PAINTING

As the term magic realism was first and principally associated with painting, it may seem an unusual choice to dedicate only a small section of this book to this form. However, as the majority of associated magic(al) realist cultural production since the coining of the term in 1925 has been in fiction, this book has concentrated predominantly on the narrative form of magical realism. This section will offer a brief explanation of the characteristics of magic realist painting and of the main artists with whom the term is associated, from the painters of the German post-expressionist movement, through the mid-twentieth-century Canadian hyper-realist movement, to the extraordinary figure of Mexican artist Frida Kahlo.

As we saw in Chapter 1, the term 'magic realism' was coined by a German art critic Franz Roh in 1925 to describe a new form of post-expressionist painting that he witnessed developing in the Weimar Republic. Producing work that attempted to portray the details of reality so vividly that it expressed the mystery of life as we witness it, the artists Otto Dix, Christian Schad, Georg Schrimpf, George Grosz and Alexander Kanoldt became, in retrospect, magic realism's most famous painters. All based in Germany between the world wars, they painted in a style that attempted to avoid all sentimentality (Guenther 1995: 35). In addition to the horror of the First World War and the slide into chaos of the Weimar Republic, the magic realist painters were influenced strongly by the work of Italian artist Giorgio de Chirico. De Chirico's work is recognized as part of the *arte metafisica* movement in Italy in the early 1910s and 1920s. His works such as *The Enigma of a Day* (1914) use a strange contrast of light and dark, often with monumental objects such as statues placed in a strangely isolated urban location almost devoid of human presence. All of this provides a bleak and disorientating atmosphere.

The magic realist artists that were influenced by De Chirico adapted his techniques by including people and nature in their paintings but retained his clarity and the bleak and disturbing atmosphere of his pictures. Franz Roh listed characteristics which he considered essential to magic realist art in a book in 1925 on post-expressionist painting; he listed twenty-two aspects that to him defined magic realist painting. In 1958, he revised this work and changed the name of this art from magic realism to 'new objectivity'. With this change, he reduced the number of artistic aspects identifying this style of painting to fifteen: 'Sober subjects, the object clarified, representational, puristically severe, static, quiet, thorough, close and far view, miniature, cold, thin paint surface, smooth, effacement of the painting process, centripetal, exernal purification of the object' (Menton 1983: 18). In 1969, another art critic, Wieland Schmied, summarized Roh's defining characteristics of magic realism in a more descriptive and helpful list:

1 Sobriety and sharp focus; an unsentimental and unemotional vision;
2 The artist's vision is directed towards the everyday, banal, insignificant subjects; the absence of timidity with regard to painting the unpleasant;
3 A static, tightly unified structure, which often suggests a completely airless, glass-like space, which, in general, gives preference to the static rather than to the dynamic;
4 The eradication of the traces of the painting process, the liberation of the painting from all signs of the handicraft;
5 And finally a new spiritual relationship with the world of things.

(Menton 1983: 26)

It is rare that such defining lists offer such a clear indication of the variety of work within a genre, but this is very much the case with magic realism, even if we consider merely those artists who produced paintings in the Weimar Republic. The work of Otto Dix (1891–1969) and of Georg Schrimpf, for instance, would be difficult to confuse. Otto Dix's painting tends to be populated with many people, no one figure having prominence over the others. His work is often described as grotesque due to the caricature-like portrayal of the people in his paintings. Some aspects of the people such as the eye-make-up or calf muscles of women in short skirts are enlarged and emphasized, producing an impression of excess. His paintings characteristically are set at night in urban surroundings, such as his triptych *Metropolis* (1927/8) which is populated by ornately dressed women, whether working or partying, and amputee soldiers crammed into small spaces. The atmosphere is stifling and sinister. The magic realist aspects of such work by Dix reside in the smoothness of the picture, the close attention to detail and the unflinching portrayal of unpleasant realities, combined with the grotesque strangeness of the peculiar mixture of closely observed people in the location.

Georg Schrimpf (1889–1938) on the other hand conforms closely to Roh's original ideas of what constituted magic realist art. His painting *Landscape in the Bavarian Forest* (1933) is of a landscape of trees in the foreground and hills in the background, with a low horizon and large expanse of sky. The effect of the perspective follows Roh's suggestion that magic realist painting should include both a far and a near view and that it should reveal the miniature. In this case, the miniature is revealed in the smallness of the landscape against the sky and the detail of the trees. The picture is almost photographic in its attention to detail and in the smoothness of the paint's surface. In fact, the magical aspect of this typically realist scene lies in the eerie accuracy of the minutely detailed trees which appear ethereal and transparent against the backdrop of the hills. This is a landscape painting which allows the viewer access to more realistic detail than their own eye would provide in one glance. It is the exaggeration of realistic detail that provides the magical atmosphere.

In later years, magic realist painting became associated with North American painters, although some painters such as Edward Hopper (1882–1967) had been painting smooth, accurate depictions of ordinary city life since the 1910s and have therefore become associated with magic realism. Hopper's paintings are realist and yet provide an atmosphere of the unreal due to his use of deep shade and his choice of obscure or overlooked subjects such as an usherette standing against a wall during a film showing in a cinema in *New York Movie* (1939) or an empty shopping street on a Sunday morning in *Early Sunday Morning* (1930). During the 1960s onwards, painters such as Alex Colville (1920–) in Canada have been called magic realist for their hyper-realistic depictions of scenes. Their magic realism follows that of Georg Schrimpf rather than Otto Dix, in that it is their photographic quality which creates a magical impression. In relation to Colville, the critic Paul Hadermann additionally points out the unusual closeness of attention to detail and proximity to the subject that provokes the view that reality is subtly being brought into question. Hadermann cites Colville's painting *To Prince Edward Island* (1965) as an example of later magic realist art. This ironically titled painting is not a landscape but the painting of a young woman looking through binoculars from the deck of a ship – presumably near Prince Edward Island. The viewpoint accentuates the size of the binoculars and, as the girl is holding them to her face and sitting leaning forward with her arms on the back of a bench, she is obscured from view except for her arms, shoulders and the outline of her face. Hadermann claims that his picture creates a spatial tension by drawing attention to the near and far of what is visible and not visible in the painting (1987: 246). The magic realism lies in the strange proximity for the viewer to such clarity and detail.

Finally, any discussion of magic realist painting would not be complete without mentioning the Mexican artist Frida Kahlo (1907–54). Some suspicion surrounds the inclusion of Kahlo amongst *magic* realists, as often her portrayals of aspects of indigenous and mixed Mexican culture leads her to be associated with the *magical* realism of García Márquez. Her paintings frequently include Mexican jewellery or artefacts as well as indigenous flora and fauna such as monkeys and parrots. However, there is a strong argument to be made for including her among magic realists according to Roh's definitions. The surfaces of her paintings are smooth and photographic and they reveal a strange juxtaposition of objects out of their context. Many of these objects are symbolic or explanatory, such as a broken column in place of her own damaged back-bone in the painting *The Broken Column* (1944), or blood vessels in the air linking two versions of herself in *The Two Fridas* (1939). However, the most frequently portrayed object in her painting is that of her own body, her self. Kahlo's work is famous for its attempt to depict herself, beyond her exterior appearance, and to explore the changes of her inner-self through the creation of her paintings. Fellow Mexican Carlos Fuentes expresses this, claiming 'Kahlo's self-portraits are beautiful for the same reason as Rembrandt's: they show us the successive identities of a human being who is not yet, but who is becoming' (1995: 16). The autobiographical element which dominates her work is the fact that she was disabled, first by polio and then by a tram accident which left her with a broken back, broken ribs, and a metal bar piercing her body through her vagina. The years of medical operations, amputations, miscarriages and pain which filled the rest of her life became the subtext of her paintings. As Fuentes summarizes, 'Her biography consists of twenty-nine years of pain' (1995: 12). Angela Carter notes in her introduction to a collection of reproduced paintings of Kahlo that:

> the accident itself, horribly, turned her into a bloody involuntary art object . . . a metal bar pierced her back; somehow all her clothes came off in the crash and the bag of gold powder carried by a fellow passenger spilled over her.
>
> (1989: 6)

In other words, the horrifically real and the extraordinary magical aspects of life are combined visually in the very image of the event that was to dominate the rest of Kahlo's life. Her face is always recognizable in her paintings, always the same from one picture to the rest with her defining single dark eyebrow across her forehead, her hair held high with an ornate Mexican comb. Kahlo in fact always appeared in public in an old-fashioned style of dress, that reflected Mexican influences, particularly in her use of jewellery, and her head-comb. In the introduction to her diaries, Fuentes describes the first time that he saw her. Her entrance into the Opera House in Mexico City drew everybody's attention due to her extraordinary appearance and the sound of her jewellery. For Fuentes, she embodies a Mexican sensibility. He explains in awe, 'It was the entrance of an Aztec goddess, perhaps Coatlicue, the mother deity wrapped in her skirt of serpents, exhibiting her own lacerated, bloody hands the way other women sport a brooch' (Fuentes 1995: 7).

It is not only her dress and the many Mexican objects which appear in her work which leads Fuentes to such a conclusion, but the fact that for him her pain and bodily mutilation is symbolic of the political damage caused by colonialism and the successive revolutions that tore the country apart. He explains, 'As the people are cleft in twain by poverty, revolution, memory, and hope, so she, the individual, the irreplaceable, the unrepeatable woman called Frida Kahlo is broken, torn inside her own body as Mexico is torn outside' (Fuentes 1995: 9). In fact, as romantic as this notion of Fuentes' may seem, Kahlo herself made a similar connection and claimed that her birth date was that of the day of Mexican independence, and hence the date of the birth of the Mexican nation (Carter 1989: 5).

According to Fuentes not only is Frida Kahlo symbolic of the nation of Mexico, but she also exemplifies Carpentier's notion that magic realism is an essential aspect of Latin America. If we consider such paintings as *Tree of Hope* (1946) we can see all of these elements at work. In the painting, the figure of Kahlo sits next to her own body on an operating table with the scars of an operation on her back exposed. Both Kahlo and her body are located in the Mexican desert, surrounded by cracks in the earth that repeat the image of the scars on her back. The repeated image indicates Kahlo's personal identification with Mexico as a geographical location and nation. Like surrealist paintings by René Magritte, the painting is divided by light and day – Kahlo sitting in night-time and her body located in the daytime. As with many of her self-portraits, the figure of Kahlo is wearing a Mexican dress and jewellery but it is further ornamented by surgical nodes. The painting at once combines the images of Kahlo and Mexico and the conflicting states of being through which she lived. With these images in mind it is not surprising that Fuentes considers that:

> Frida Kahlo remains . . . the most powerful reminder that what the French Surrealists codified has always been an everyday reality in Mexico and Latin America, part of the cultural stream, a spontaneous fusing of myth and fact, dream and vigil, reason and fantasy.
>
> (1995: 14)

To this day, Kahlo has remained the most prominent magic realist painter and has in fact overshadowed the prominence of magic realist painters of the Weimar Republic. As with magical realist literature, it is Latin America which has become the most recognized location of magic realist painting, despite its origins in German post-expressionism.

7

THE FUTURE OF MAGIC(AL) REALISM

This book has dispelled the idea that the terms 'magic realism', 'magical realism' and 'marvellous realism' should be dismissed simply because their histories and application have been complicated. What the future of the terms will be is a matter of speculation except that at some time or other most literary terms have undergone changes of meaning, if they have not been forgotten altogether. As magical realism has been so very fashionable during the last few decades of the twentieth century, its survival as a recognized and popular narrative mode of writing into the twenty-first century is somewhat under threat as fashions change.

There are three major points of disagreement with the term magical realism among critics. Many consider that the over-association of magical realism with Latin America has led to it being seen as a passing fashion in the literary history of a certain region, and its application elsewhere as a tired and borrowed cliché. For example, the Latin American cultural critic John King wrote a book in 1990 on Latin American film titled *Magical Reels*. Although King's book did not consider magical realism in film, he saw the title as one that would draw the reader and ironically reflect the late twentieth-century assumption that everything Latin American must be magical realist. For King, the title served to

> cut through the myths of utopia and dystopia which have surrounded
> the continent since it was originally 'named' by *conquistadors* and
> chroniclers in the sixteenth century and which have their most recent
> incarnation in the sloppy use of the term 'magical realist' by western
> critics eager to bracket and to explain away the cultural production of
> the region.
>
> (1990: 5)

This may have been an ironic move on his part, but in fact it is double-edged in that it increases the association of magical realism with Latin America even further. Of course, any other careful study of the term can identify the qualities of the narrative mode that make it so very appealing to so many cross-cultural and postcolonial writers outside Latin America, and provide opposition to John King's assumptions.

The two further criticisms of magical realism are less easy to counter. They are both related to the subversive and transgressive political possibilities of magical realism as outlined in Chapter 4. Several critics, such as Liam Connell, Brenda Cooper and Timothy Brennan, have noted that the adoption of magical realism in order to create postcolonial discourse can rely too heavily on the writer's assumption of a Western perspective. Stephen Slemon's explanation of the relationship of postcolonialism and magical realism discussed in Chapter 5 helps to clarify their objections. It follows that if magical realism is constructed from the conflicting discourses of the magical and the realist, and if this model is then associated with the postcolonial situation in which the colonized and the colonialist are forever in conflict, then one or other of the two may appear to be associated with the 'magical' and the other with the 'realist'. As Connell explains, it is the attempt to carry out a study of the form of magical realist narrative that brings studies to such a jarring conclusion: 'Formal definitions of Magic Realism fundamentally depend on the dissimilarity of the two modes of thinking because they have tended to focus on an effect derived from the incongruity of myth and rationalism' (1998: 103). The implication of this is that the model replicates colonialist thinking in its affirmation of the 'primitive' and pre-modern attributes of the colonized, whereas the colonialists are a people whose culture is rational, progressive and modern. Connell indicates that such a view carries further damaging implications. He explains that:

As James Clifford has argued, in *The Predicament of Culture*, that interest in 'traditional' art forms tends to locate such art production as anterior, as existing prior to, and without reference to, the modern world. Not only does this obscure the fact that art is still being made by such peoples, but it also serves to locate 'tribal' people in a non-historical time and ourselves [as westerners] in a different historical time.

(Connell 1998: 101)

In colonialist terms, the binary opposition of the magical and the realist, places more value on realism and pragmatism than it does on the magical which it associates negatively with the irrational. It again reinforces the colonialist view that the colonized are like irrational children who need the guidance and superior knowledge of the colonial power in order to progress into modernity. Liam Connell notes that this is exacerbated by many magical realist writers who purposefully choose to set their stories in non-Western cultures that resist modernization. A text such as *One Hundred Years of Solitude* by García Márquez is an excellent example of this. Rather than setting his novel in the urban landscape of Bogotá, or in the industrial landscapes of Colombia, he sets his novel in the past, in an isolated community whose cultural belief system is a mixture of Amerindian myths and Christian and rural suspicion. As Connell points out, much of *One Hundred Years of Solitude* relies on the alien and seemingly miraculous scientific discoveries presented to them by the magician Melquíades (1998: 98). Of course, as we have seen from our discussion in Chapter 5, this can be what constitutes these texts' subversive power. Despite writing in the Western form of the novel, these texts present other ways of looking at the world than are presented through Western realism. Moreover, cross-cultural magical realists such as Toni Morrison avoid such a situation by creating an integrated magical realist discourse in their novels, that does not rely on the friction between the magical and the real, but rather, is an amalgamation of the two ways of thinking.

Brenda Cooper also recognizes this third way of seeing things in relation to the West African magical realist writing of Ben Okri and Amos Tutuola. However, Cooper also notes the complexity of the cosmopolitan writer's relationship to the non-Western pre- (or non-) scientific aspects of the magical realist text. Cooper claims that the non-scientific magical point of view must be dealt with in a respectful way by the writer, despite the writer's sophistication and modern education. She explains that 'This dignity can only evolve if there is a lack of patronization, which is itself dependent on genuine faith in, and respect for, the beliefs portrayed' and yet:

> What is always the case, however, is that it is neither possible nor appropriate for magical realist writers to present in an unmediated, undistanced way, the pre-scientific view of the world that some of the characters may hold. The gulf between the peasant's and the writer's point of view is a critical space where the negotiations between magic and realism take place.
>
> (Cooper 1998: 33)

The assumed 'gulf' between the perspectives of the peasantry about which the books are written and the writers themselves has been the focus of critical opposition to the magical realist novels of Rushdie and García Márquez. Both writers are seen by Cooper and the postcolonial critic Timothy Brennan as belonging to a cosmopolitan, educated and literate class who have little experience of the illiterate and local underclass that they portray. Cooper asks of Rushdie 'Why does he post the existence of "something in common" with other Third World countries . . . and simultaneously retreat from such an identification with the disclaimer that he has nothing "as simplistic as a united 'third world' outlook?"' (1998: 18).

In Brennan's opinion, both Rushdie and García Márquez are removed from the actual material difficulties of living with the after-effects of colonialism, and are protected from poverty and prejudice by virtue of their education and social status. Both writers were educated in European and Western thought and literature, and have (despite Rushdie's *fatwa*) high levels of personal freedom. They appear to be 'citizens of the world', influenced by Western ideology and ideas of globalization. The effect of this is that, according to Brennan, both writers do portray the kind of patronizing attitude towards the illiterate classes that Cooper warns against. Moreover, for Brennan, their distance from the actual suffering of the 'subaltern' postcolonial people that they seek to represent means that the treatment of the aftermath of colonialism in their writing is flippant. This is compounded by the inclusion of magical happenings. Thus, Brennan proposes that Rushdie and García Márquez reinforce western, colonialist attitudes despite their attempts to counter them: 'Their shockingly inappropriate juxtaposition of humorous, matter-of-factness and appallingly accurate violence, both ironically alludes to the blasé reporting of contemporary news and the preventable horrors of current events' (1989: 69). Ultimately, it is their seeming lack of commitment to anti-colonialism and sympathy with western colonialism that most offends Timothy Brennan, who states:

> Both García Márquez and Rushdie . . . temper and subvert the routine appeals by writers of anti-colonial commitment to 'native' discourse by showing not only the inevitability but the benefits of what has been left behind. Their discourse, instead of telling a story reviling Europeans for their dishonourable past, stylistically alludes to that past and appropriates it for their own use.
>
> (1989: 69)

In the context of existing criticism, Brennan takes an extreme position against the work of Rushdie and García Márquez. The Indian critic Kum Kum Sangari is more understanding of Rushdie's position, noting that the style of his writing and his insider/outsider standpoint in relation to postcolonial India is a reflection of his own social position: 'In some sense Rushdie represents a postcolonial middle-class ethos and is shaped by its contradictions' (1987: 177).

Liam Connell also presents a more moderate critique of the work of García Márquez but also has some sympathy with the ideas of Brennan. He warns critics, 'It is important also to be vigilant against making the mistake of thinking that just because García Márquez is Colombian, he believes in the myths that he uses' (Connell 1998: 107). Connell considers García Márquez to position himself at a distance from magical realism and by doing so appears to develop a patronizing stance. However, whilst his point may be a good warning to the reader and critic in general, his reference to García Márquez seems weaker when we consider that the writer himself claims that he does indeed believe the myths he includes (and similar ways of thinking passed on to him from his grandmother).

Here, we are confronted with the choice of believing or not believing what the writer claims about himself and his writing.

One of the main strengths of an argument such as that of Connell's, Brennan's and Cooper's, is that they recognize that it is not simply the writer's context that determines the appropriateness of the adoption of a magical realist perspective but that the reception of the text by the reader must also be considered. The objection that many critics raise against magical realism is that it is a very popular fictional form among western readers who are not familiar with the world which it depicts. This highlights several concerns: is it popular because it offers an exotic notion of life in the Third World; is it popular because it provides a means of escaping reality; is it popular because, according to critics such as Brennan and Connell, it can reinforce colonial thinking? These critics assume that a western educated readership has been schooled in colonialist thinking (whether directly or indirectly, consciously or subconsciously), and in the thinking of the Enlightenment. With these assumptions in mind, Cooper notes that it is difficult for a Western reader to accept fully the dignity of a non-scientific belief system as portrayed in a magical realist novel. She cites the problem of 'the almost inevitable, simultaneous scepticism of Western educated writers who assume an ironic distance from the lack of a "scientific" understanding. This they do paradoxically while celebrating the so-called authenticity of superstition' (Cooper 1998: 33). There is an implication in such an analysis that western readers are unable to read beyond their own context, and in fact, when they do read texts that are set in non-scientific and non-pragmatic cultural contexts, then they read in order to enter an escapist fantasy world that they do not register as 'reality'. Cooper claims that this is one of the contradictions of magical realism:

> Magical realism attempts to capture reality by way of a depiction of life's many dimensions, seen and unseen, visible and invisible, rational and mysterious. In the process, such writers walk a political tightrope between capturing this reality and providing precisely the exotic escape from reality desired by some of their Western readership.
>
> (1998: 32)

From some perspectives, such as that of Brennan, such escapism provided by non-realist postcolonial works is a means to reinforce a denial of the effects of colonialism and the related problems of the Third World. Here, Brennan again attacks Rushdie for utilizing the potentially liberating narrative focus of magical realism and adapting it for a Western readership. He calls this the 'The Anglicisation of "magical realism"' and associates it with a 'saleable "Third Worldism"' (Brennan 1989: 65). In other words, he considers Rushdie to have begun a process of emptying magical realism of its radical political possibilities in order to appeal to the large Western (and rich) readership.

As for the political possibilities of magical realism, the adoption of the technique by postcolonial writers does point to its acceptance as a liberating and transformative narrative mode. However, the fundamentalist Muslim interpretation of Rushdie's *The Satanic Verses* which led to a *fatwa* being declared against him in 1989, reveals exactly the problem of assuming that all readers are open to the positive fictional qualities of magical realism. Rushdie was accused of creating blasphemous references to Islam by re-writing passages of the Koran. Some critics also point to the fact that he caricatures the Ayatollah Khomeini in his text. Rushdie's defence was that his work was fictional and literary, and was concerned with the idea of the transmission and transcription of scriptures as an act of literary creation. Like the magical realist writing of Angela Carter, Rushdie's work could be interpreted in the European tradition of the carnivalesque whereby the sacred is treated as profane and the profane as sacred. This reversal of order reinforces sanctity by releasing the tension and giving voice temporarily and in a controlled setting to the profane. Brenda Cooper sees the argument posed in broader terms; Islamic fundamentalism versus Western postmodernism. As she explains, for the cosmopolitan and migrant Rushdie 'hybridity is a new way of life' whereas for fundamentalists it is 'heresy' (Cooper 1998: 21). For Cooper, it is the very multiple and hybrid quality of Rushdie's magical realism which, when combined with elements of Islam, created a problematic text.

Again this problem resides in the unpredictability of the reader's reception of magical realism. Although careful critical consideration and writing may help to reduce this problem in academia in the future, the majority of the reading public have little contact with literary criticism. It seems that unless the reading public are aware of colonialism, its attitudes and its aftermath, then the possibility to take an exotic or escapist approach to magical realist narratives will remain.

Ultimately, the problems of magical realism are inherent in its contradictory and multi-perspectival form and this may, in the future, be its nemesis. As it does not impose a judgemental attitude towards either its realist or magical aspects, it allows itself to be open to multiple interpretations, and this possibly includes those that oppose diversity. Its liberating and transformative powers are latent in the work, and yet can only be activated by the act of reading or viewing by a sympathetic public. This form of art relies more than most upon the belief, the perspective and the willingness to change those beliefs and perspectives of the reader or viewer. Magical realism is an intimate affair between the reader/viewer and the text/film. As such, its future as a particular and identifiable narrative mode is vulnerable, but at the very least, discussion of magic(al) realism during the past eighty years has opened up the debate concerning the relationship between reality and fiction, and the reader's/viewer's role within that relationship. Far from being simply a fashionable narrative device, magic(al) realism has proved itself through the criticism it has generated to stimulate consideration of the relationship of fiction and representation to reality.

GLOSSARY

Allegory A narrative that has two levels of meaning – the one of the plot, and the other of a covert alternative meaning. In allegorical writing, the plot tends to be subsumed by the importance of the alternative meaning.

Avant-garde A movement of radical experimentation in the Arts that is most closely associated with the modernist period of the late nineteenth to the mid-twentieth centuries.

The boom A period of prolific literary production in 1950s and 1960s Latin America. The fiction of this period became known as the 'new novel' and is generally considered to be modernist. The writers associated with the boom sought to break away from previous literary traditions and to find a new means of expression. It is frequently associated with novelistic experimentation and magical realism.

Carnivalesque A term introduced to literary theory by the mid-twentieth century Russian critic Mikhail Bakhtin referring to the challenge to authority instigated by the temporary reversal of social order. Although the challenge to authority appears to be revolutionary, Bakhtin emphasizes that the revolutionary moment is only temporary and provides a release of class tension that allows the reinstatement and maintenance of the same social order. It is based on a study of medieval religious carnival in which the sacred and profane are inverted. The term is discussed at length by Bakhtin in his studies *Rabelais and his World* and *Problems of Dostoevsky's Poetics*.

Criollo The Spanish term which is equivalent to the English term 'creole'. This term is subject to a wide variety of nuances but essentially refers to a mixed cultural heritage. In the sense used by magical realist critics such as Alejo Carpentier, the term refers to Caribbean people of mixed race and culture, particularly those of mixed African and Spanish heritage. This is not to be confused with the fact that in English colonial White European residents of the Carribean were also called 'creole'. *Mestizaje* refers to a mixed cultural or racial heritage which includes indigenous American cultural influences.

Cross-culturalism A term referring to the commingle of cultural influences or elements, e.g. African American. It is different from multi-culturalism which refers to the coexistance of distinct cultural elements and trans-culturalism which refers to the crossing of one cultural element into another cultural context.

Dialogic discourse See **Heteroglossia**.

Epistemological magical realism A term introduced by Roberto González Echevarría in 1974 to distinguish a kind of magical realism in which the magical element is derived from aspects of knowledge rather than from cultural belief, e.g. the existence of a computer with a personality such as that in Amitav Ghosh's *The Calcutta Chromosome*. This form of magical realism does not rely on the existence of a tradition of belief in such a magical element in order for the magical realism to come into play. It is derived from the distinction between the philosophical study of those things pertaining to knowledge (epistemology) and the study of those things pertaining to belief (ontology).

The fantastic The fantastic is a genre of art and literature in which there is a constant faltering between belief and non-belief in the supernatural or extraordinary events presented. The critic Tzvetan Todorov identifies the key characteristic of the fantastic as the reader's hesitation between natural and supernatural explanations for the fictional events in the text.

Feminism Feminism is a political attitude and movement that calls for the status, rights and desires of women to be taken into consideration in all aspects of life. It came to prominence at the end of the eighteenth century, again in the mid-nineteenth century and gained in popularity and force towards the end of the twentieth century. In literary criticism, feminism is an approach to reading and criticism that focuses on the experiences of women in fiction, attitudes towards women in fiction, the status of women's writing and differing approaches, methods and language use adopted by women writers in comparison to those of men.

Genre A term referring to a particular category of literary text, following a particular format or convention such as 'the novel' or 'science fiction'.

Heteroglossia A term referring to the existence of more than one voice or language. It is frequently used in literary criticism with particular reference to Mikhail Bakhtin's theories of narrative and discourse that distinguish between the voices of the narrator and the characters of a novel. It is related to Bakhtin's theory of dialogic discourse which examines the positive effects of heteroglossia where there are competing voices in a text.

Magic realism   A term introduced in 1925 referring to art that attempts to produce a clear depiction of reality that includes a presentation of the mysterious elements of everyday life.

Magic realization of metaphor   A term coined by the critic Marguerite Alexander in reference to Salman Rushdie's literal enactment in his texts of metaphors and expressions so that, for instance, a character will literally burn when in a state of passion.

Magical realism   A term introduced in the 1940s referring to narrative art that presents extraordinary occurrences as an ordinary part of everyday reality.

Magic(al) realism   An umbrella term used in this book when discussing the artistic concept that encapsulates aspects of both magic realism and magical realism.

Marvellous realism   A term similar to magical realism but used in reference specifically to Latin American. It is translated from the Spanish term *lo realismo maravilloso* that was coined in Latin America in the 1940s to refer to narrative art that presents the mystical and magical elements as an integral part of everyday reality in Latin America.

Marxism   A study or philosophy derived from the ideas of the nineteenth-century philosopher Karl Marx. In literary study such an approach focuses attention on what the text relays to us about social structures and frequently involves the criticism of a text from a left-wing socialist position.

Meta-fiction   A form of fiction that includes the contemplation of aspects of literature and fiction such as a novel about writing a novel. These texts are often considered to be self-reflexive.

Modernism   A term referring to a cultural movement that has been very broadly applied to culture after industrialization or more narrowly to experimental art and literature of the early twentieth century that attempted to create new ways of expressing reality. In literature in English it is often associated with the works of James Joyce, Virginia Woolf and Wallace Stevens.

New novel See **The boom**.

Ontological magical realism A term developed from 'ontology'. It is a variant of magical realism whose magical aspects are in accordance with the cultural beliefs of the context in which the fiction is set or written.

Ontology The philosophical study of those things related to belief.

Postcolonialism A term that refers to both the political situation of a previously colonized country after independence and/or to a philosophy and form of cultural criticism that exposes and opposes imperialism.

Post-expressionism An art movement following that of expressionism, usually associated with German painting. Early twentieth-century post-expressionist art attempts to depict a clear representation of life without sentimentality while also including its mystical aspects. This is differentiated from expressionist art which attempts to depict the reality of emotion without concern for the accurate representation of surface reality.

Postmodernism A term that has been broadly applied to the period following the 1940s and also more specifically to architecture, art and literature that takes forms, tropes and elements from previous eras and reconstructs them as pastiche or with irony. It is frequently associated with post-structuralism and self-reflexivity as it is a form of architecture, art and literature that self-consciously exposes its structures.

Post-structuralism A form of late twentieth-century literary theory that challenges structuralist assumptions, rejects Marxist ideas and emphasizes multiple interpretations of texts. Structuralism, advanced by the linguist Ferdinand de Saussure, sought to explain the way in which words and meaning are linked through a stable system of communicable signs. In reaction to this, post-structuralism, propounded by the philosopher Jacques Derrida, sought to reveal the instability of the system and the reliance of the system of language upon 'difference'. The deconstruction of Saussure's system of language in literary criticism, such as that by Roland Barthes, emphasizes the role of each individual reader in the production of multiple meanings and identifies a lack of an authoritative interpretation of meaning for the text.

Realism In literature, the term 'realism' refers to the attempt to create an accurate depiction of actual life. Although originally a philosophical term, in the mid-nineteenth century it came into common use referring to the writer's creation of a believable fictive world. This approach to the experience of life relies upon the belief that it is possible to gain a faithful picture of reality through one's senses and to communicate this to another. In the twentieth century, as faith in the abilities of perception and communication were being questioned, debate concerning 'realism' focused on the process by which the illusion of reality is created.

Self-reflexive A narrative or narrator referring to, or drawing attention to, itself or himself thereby making the reader aware of the narrator's role in the text.

Surrealism An artistic movement that lasted from 1919 to 1939 that attempted to find ways to explore human psychology and to express the sub-conscious and unconscious. It was defined by its practitioners through a manifesto written in 1924 by the French writer, and most famous literary surrealist, André Breton. Following the trauma of the First World War, surrealism sought a break from the old order and to develop new ways of thinking, particularly in relation to primitive aspects of human existence.

Transgression The crossing of a boundary or line, the breaking of a regulation or social more. This term has come to be used frequently in feminist criticism in relation to the rejection of and active opposition to socially constructed social roles for women.

Trope A figure of speech or use of language such as a metaphor.

BIBLIOGRAPHY

MAGIC(AL) REALIST PRIMARY SOURCES

Allende, Isabel [1982] (1986) *The House of the Spirits*, trans. Magda Bogin, London: Black Swan.

Anderson-Dargatz, Gail [1996] (1998) *The Cure for Death by Lightning*, London: Virago.

Asturias, Miguel Angel [1949] (1988) *Men of Maize*, trans. Gerald Martin, London: Verso.

Bond, Michael [1958] (2001) *A Bear Called Paddington*, London: Collins.

Borges, Jorge Luis [1935] (1975) *A Universal History of Infamy*, trans. Norman Thomas di Giovanni, Harmondsworth, Middlesex: Penguin.

Brautigan, Richard [1967] (1989) *Trout Fishing in America*, Boston, MA: Houghton Mifflin.

Brink, André [1996] (2000a) *Imaginings of Sand*, London: Vintage.

—— [1999] (2000b) *Devil's Valley: A Novel*, London: Vintage.

Bulgakov, Mikhail [1967] (1984) *The Master and Margarita*, trans. Michael Glenny, London: Flamingo/Fontana.

Calvino, Italo [1957] (1980a) 'The Baron in the Trees', trans. Archibald Colquhuon, in *Our Ancestors*, London: Picador, pp. 77–284.

—— [1957] (1980b) 'Introduction', trans. Isabel Quigly, in *Our Ancestors*, London: Picador, pp. vii–x.

Carpentier, Alejo [1949] (1975) *The Kingdom of this World*, trans. Harriet de Onis, Harmondsworth, Middlesex: Penguin.

Carter, Angela [1991] (1992) *Wise Children*, London: Vintage.

—— [1984] (1994) *Nights at the Circus*, London: Vintage.

Castillo, Ana [1993] (1994) *So Far From God*, London: Women's Press.

Dahl, Roald [1988] (2001) *Matilda*, London: Penguin.

Daisne, Johan [1942] (1943) *De trap van steen en wolken*, Brussels: Manteau.

Esquivel, Laura [1989] (1993) *Like Water for Chocolate*, trans. Carol Christensen and Thomas Christensen, London: Black Swan.

García Márquez, Gabriel [1967] (1972) *One Hundred Years of Solitude*, trans. Gregory Rabassa, London: Penguin.

—— [1975] (1978) *The Autumn of the Patriarch*, trans. Gregory Rabassa, London: Picador.

—— [1981] (1982a) *Chronicle of a Death Foretold*, trans. Gregory Rabassa, London: Cape.

—— (1982b) 'The Solitude of Latin America: Nobel Lecture', trans. Marina Castañeda, in Julio Ortega (ed.) *Gabriel García Márquez and the Powers of Fiction*, Austin: University of Texas Press.

Ghosh, Amitav [1995] (1997) *The Calcutta Chromosome: A Novel of Fevers, Delerium and Discovery*, Toronto: Vintage Canada.

Grass, Günther [1959] (1965) *The Tin Drum*, trans. Ralph Mannheim, Harmondsworth, Middlesex: Penguin.

Harris, Wilson (1996) *Jonestown*, London: Faber and Faber.

—— [1960] (1998) *Palace of the Peacock*, London: Faber and Faber.

Hodgins, Jack [1977] (1986) *The Invention of the World*, Toronto: Macmillan.

Hong Kingston, Maxine [1976] (1981a) *The Woman Warrior: Memoirs of a Girlhood Among Ghosts*, London: Picador.

—— [1980] (1981b) *China Men*, London: Picador.

—— [1989] (1990) *Tripmaster Monkey: His Fake Book*, New York: Vintage.

Irving, John [1978] (1999) *The World According to Garp*, London: Black Swan.

Kroetsch, Robert (1978) *What the Crow Said*, Don Mills, Ontario: General Publishing.

—— (1980) *The Crow Journals*, Edmonton: NeWest Press.

—— (1989) 'The Moment of the Discovery of America Continues', in *The Lovely Treachery of Words: Essays Selected and New*, Toronto: Oxford University Press, pp. 1–20.

Lampo, Hubert [1960] (1974a) *The Coming of Joachim Stiller*, trans. Marga Emlyn-Jones, New York: Twayne.

—— [1969] (1974b) *Kaspar in de onderwereld: of De goden moeten hun getal hebben*, Amsterdam: Meulenhoff.

MacDonald, Ann-Marie (1996) *Fall on Your Knees*, Toronto: Knopf Canada.

Melville, Pauline (1990) *Shape-Shifter: Stories*, London: Women's Press.

—— [1997] (1998) *The Ventriloquist's Tale*, London: Bloomsbury.

—— [1998] (1999) *The Migration of Ghosts*, London: Bloomsbury.

Morrison, Toni [1987] (1988) *Beloved*, London: Picador.

—— [1977] (1989) *Song of Solomon*, London: Picador.

—— [1992] (1993) *Jazz*, London: Picador.

Nesbit, E. [1902] (1979) *Five Children and It* [1904] *The Phoenix and the Carpet* and *The Story of the Amulet*, London: Octopus.

Norton, Mary [1947] (1970) *Bedknob and Broomstick*, London: Penguin.

Okri, Ben [1991] (1992) *The Famished Road*, London: Vintage.

Ondaatje, Michael (1982) *Running in the Family*, Toronto: Maclelland and Stewart.

Pynchon, Thomas [1966] (1979) *The Crying of Lot 49*, London: Picador.

Roy, Arundhati (1997) *The God of Small Things*, London: Flamingo.

Rushdie, Salman [1981] (1982) *Midnight's Children*, London: Picador.

—— [1983] (1984) *Shame*, London: Picador.

—— (1991) *Imaginary Homelands: Essays and Criticism (1981–1991)*, London: Granta.

—— [1988] (1992) *The Satanic Verses*, Dover, Delaware: Consortium.

Silko, Leslie Marmon [1991] (1992) *The Almanac of the Dead: A Novel*, New York: Penguin.

Süskind, Patrick [1985] (1987) *Perfume: The Story of a Murderer*, trans. John E. Woods, London: Penguin.

Thompson, Hunter S [1971] (1993) *Fear and Loathing in Las Vegas: A Savage Journey to the Heart of the American Dream*, London: Flamingo/HarperCollins.
Tutuola, Amos (1952) *The Palm-Wine Drinkard*, London: Faber.
White, E. B. [1945] (1969) *Stuart Little*, Harmondsworth, Middlesex: Puffin/Hamish Hamilton.

Films

Arau, Alfonso (1992) *Como agua para chocolate*, Mexico: Arau Films International/ IMCINE/CONACULTA/SECTUR.
Capra, Frank (1946) *It's a Wonderful Life*, United States of America: Liberty Films.
Jonze, Spike (1999) *Being John Malkovich*, United States of America: Universal.
Siberling, Brad (1997) *City of Angels*, United States of America: Warner.
Wenders, Wim (1987) *Der Himmel über Berlin/Wings of Desire*, Berlin: Road Movies Film Produktion and Paris: Argos Films.
Minkoff, Robert (1999) *Stuart Little*, United States of America: Columbia Pictures.

Paintings

Colville, Alex (1965) *To Prince Edward Island*, National Gallery of Canada, Ottawa.
Dix, Otto (1920) *Match Seller I*, Staatsgalerie, Stuttgart.
—— (1927/8) *Metropolis*, Galerie der Stadt, Stuttgart.
De Chirico, Giorgio (1914) *The Enigma of the Day*, Museum of Modern Art, New York.
Grosz, George (1921) *Gray Day*, Staatliche Museen zu Berlin–Preussischer Kulturbesitz, Nationalgalerie, Berlin.
Hopper, Edward (1930) *Early Sunday Morning*, Whitney Museum of American Art, New York.
—— (1939) *New York Movie*, Museum of Modern Art, New York.
Kahlo, Frida (1939) *The Two Fridas*, Museo d'arte moderne, Mexico City.
—— (1944) *The Broken Column*, Museo Dolores, Olmedao Patino.
—— (1946) *Tree of Hope*, Isadore Ducasse Fine Arts, New York.
Kandolt, Alexander (1926) *Still Life II*, Staatliche Kunstsammlungen, Gemäldegalerie Neue Meister, Dresden.
Schrimpf, Georg (1933) *Landscape in the Bavarian Forest*, Bayerische Staats-gemäldesammlungen, Munich.

MAGIC(AL) REALIST SECONDARY SOURCES

Alexander, Marguerite (1994) 'Salman Rushdie and "the Real World"', unpublished.
Andrews, Jennifer (1999) 'Rethinking the Relevance of Magic Realism for English-

Canadian Literature: Reading Ann-Marie MacDonald's Fall on Your Knees', *Studies in Canadian Literature/Etudes en literature Canadienne*, **24**, 1: 1–19.

Angulo, Maria-Elena (1995) *Magic Realism: Social Context and Discourse*, New York: Garland.

Borges, Jorge Luis (1961) '*El arte narrativo y la magia*', *Discusi nar*, Buenos Aires: Emecé.

Carpentier, Alejo [1949] (1995a) 'On the Marvelous Real in America', trans. Tanya Huntington and Lois Parkinson Zamora, in Lois Parkinson Zamora and Wendy B. Faris (eds) *Magical Realism: Theory, History, Community*, Durham, NC London: Duke University Press, pp. 75–88.

—— [1975] (1995b) 'The Baroque and the Marvelous Real', trans. Tanya Huntington and Lois Parkinson Zamora, in Lois Parkinson Zamora and B. Wendy Faris (eds) *Magical Realism: Theory, History, Community*, Durham, NC and London: Duke University Press, pp. 89–108.

Chanady, Amaryll Beatrice (1985) *Magical Realism and the Fantastic: Resolved Versus Unresolved Antinomy*, New York: Garland.

Connell, Liam (1998) 'Discarding Magic Realism: Modernism, Anthropology, and Critical Practice', *ARIEL: A Review of International English Literature* **29**, 2 (April): 95–110.

Cooper, Brenda (1998) *Magical Realism in West African Fiction: Seeing with a Third Eye*, London: Routledge.

Dash, J. Michael (1974) 'Marvellous Realism – the Way Out of Négritude', *Caribbean Studies*, **13**, 4 (January): 57–70.

Delbaere, Jeanne (1992) 'Magic Realism: The Energy of the Margins', in Theo D'Haen and Hans Bertens (eds) *Postmodern Fiction in Canada*, Amsterdam: Rodopi.

—— (1995) 'Psychic Realism, Mythic Realism, Grotesque Realism: Variations on Magic Realism in Contemporary Literature in English', in Lois Parkinson Zamora and Wendy B. Faris (eds) *Magical Realism: Theory, History, Community*, Durham, NC and London: Duke University Press, pp. 249–63.

Dupuis, Michel (1987) 'Flandre et Pays-bas', in Jean Weisgerber (ed.) *Le Réalisme Magique: Roman, Peinture et Cinéma*, Cahiers des avants-gardes series, Brussels: Centre d'Etude des Avants-Gardes Littéraires de l'Université de Bruxelles.

Durix, Jean Pierre (1998) *Mimesis, Genres and Postcolonial Discourse: Deconstructing Magic Realism*, Houndmills, Basingstoke: Macmillan.

Drury, Roger W (1977) 'Realism Plus Fantasy Equals Magic', in Paul Heins (ed.) *Crosscurrents of Criticism: Horn Book Essays 1968–1977*, Boston, MA: Horn Books.

Echevarría, Roberto González (1974) 'Isla a su vuela fugitiva: Carpentier y el realismo mágico', *Revista Iberoamericana*, **40**, 86: 35.

—— (1977) *Alejo Carpentier: The Pilgrim at Home*, Ithaca, NY and London: Cornell University Press.

Faris, Wendy B (1995) 'Scheherezade's Children: Magical Realism and Postmodern Fiction', in Lois Parkinson Zamora and Wendy Faris (eds) *Magical Realism:*

Theory, History, Community, Durham, NC and London: Duke University Press, pp. 163–90.

Flores, Angel [1955] (1995) 'Magical Realism in Spanish American Fiction', in Lois Parkinson Zamora and Wendy Faris (eds) *Magical Realism: Theory, History, Community*, Durham, NC and London: Duke University Press, pp. 109–17.

Foreman, P. Gabrielle (1995) 'Past-On Stories: History and the Magically Real, Morrison and Allende on Call', in Lois Parkinson Zamora and Wendy Faris (eds) *Magical Realism: Theory, History, Community*, Durham, NC and London: Duke University Press, pp. 285–303.

García Márquez, Gabriel and Mario Vargas Llosa (1967) *La novella en America Latina, Dialogo*, Lima: Universidad Nacional de Ingenieria.

Guenther, Irene (1995) "Magic Realism, New Objectivity, and the Arts during the Weimar Republic", in Lois Parkinson Zamora and Wendy Faris (eds) *Magical Realism: Theory, History, Community*, Durham, NC and London: Duke University Press, pp. 33–73.

Hadermann, Paul (1987) 'Le Réalisme Magique en Peinture', in Jean Weisgerber (ed.) *Le Réalisme Magique: Roman, Peinture et Cinéma*, Cahiers des avants-gardes series, Brussels: Centre d'Etude des Avants-Gardes Littéraires de l'Université de Bruxelles, pp. 245–61.

Hancock, Geoff (ed.) (1980) 'Introduction', in *Magic Realism*, Toronto: Aya Press: 7–15.

Hart, Patricia (1989) *Narrative Magic in the Fiction of Isabel Allende*, Cranbury, NJ: Associated University Presses.

Irish, James (1970) 'Magical Realism: A Search for Caribbean and Latin American Roots', *Literary Half-Yearly* (University of Mysore), 11, 2: 127–39, p. 128.

Jameson, Fredric (1986) 'On Magic Realism in Film', *Critical Inquiry*, 12, Winter: 301–25.

Lampo, Hubert (1993) *De Wortels der Verbeelding: De Wroclaw Colleges Over het Magisch-realisme*, Amsterdam: Meulenhoff/Antwerp: Manteau.

Menton, Seymour (1983) *Magic Realism Rediscovered, 1918–1981*, Philadelphia: Art Alliance/London and Toronto: Associated University Presses.

—— (1998) *Historia verdadera del realismo magico*, Mexico: Fondo de Cultura Economica.

Merivale, Patricia (1995) 'Saleem Fathered by Oskar: *Midnight's Children*, Magic Realism, and *The Tin Drum*', in *Magical Realism: Theory, History , Community*, Durham, NC and London: Duke University Press, pp. 329–45.

Michalski, Sergiusz (1994) *New Objectivity: Painting, Graphic Art and Photography in Weimar Germany, 1919–1933*, Cologne: Benedikt Taschen.

Nikolajeva, Maria (1988) *The Magic Code: the Use of Magical Patterns in Fantasy for Children*, Stockholm: Almqvist and Wiksell.

Roh, Franz (1925) *Nach-Expressionismus, Magischer Realismus: Probleme der neusten europäischen Malerei*, Leipzig: Klinkhardt und Biermann.

—— (1927) *Realismo mágico, post expresionismo: Problemas de la pintura europea mas reciente*, trans. Fernando Vela, Madrid: Revista de Occidente.

—— (1968) *German Art in the Twentieth Century: Painting, Sculpture, Architecture*, with additions by Juliane Roh, London: Thames and Hudson.

—— [1927] (1995) 'Magic Realism: Post-Expressionism', trans. Wendy B. Faris, in Lois Parkinson Zamora and Wendy B. Faris (eds) *Magical Realism: Theory, History, Community*, Durham, NC and London: Duke University Press, pp. 15–31.

Sangari, Kum Kum (1987) 'The Politics of the Possible', *Cultural Critique*, **7**, Fall, 157–86.

Silko, Leslie Marmon (1997) *Yellow Woman and the Beauty of the Spirit: Essays on Native American Life Today*, New York: Simon and Schuster.

Slemon, Stephen [1988] (1995) 'Magic Realism as Postcolonial Discourse', in Lois Parkinson Zamora and Wendy B. Faris (eds) *Magical Realism: Theory, History, Community*, Durham, NC and London: Duke University Press, pp. 407–26.

Smith, Louisa (1996) 'Real Gardens with Imaginary Toads: Domestic Fantasy', in Peter Hunt (ed.) *International Companion Encyclopedia of Children's Literature*, London and New York: Routledge, pp. 295–302.

Ten Kortenaar, Neil (1995) '*Midnight's Children* and the Allegory of History', *Ariel: A Review of International English Literature*, **26**, 2: 41–61.

Weisberger, Jean (ed.) (1987) *Le Réalisme Magique: Roman, Peinture et Cinéma*, Cahiers des avants-gardes series, Brussels: Centre d'Etude des Avants-Gardes Littéraires de l'Université de Bruxelles.

Wenzel, Marita (2002) 'Integrations and Mutations in Recent South African Writing with Specific Reference to André Brink's *Imaginings of Sand* and *Devil's Valley*', in Isabel Hoving, Kathleen Gyssels and Maggie Ann Bowers (eds) *Convergences and Interferences: Newness in Intercultural Practices/Ecritures d'une nouvelle ère/aire*, Amsterdam: Rodopi.

Zamora, Lois and Wendy B. Faris (1995) *Magical Realism: Theory, History, Community*, Durham, NC and London: Duke University Press.

Other Cited Sources

Achebe, Chinua (1973) *Arrow of God*, London: Heinemann.

Aristotle (1920) *Poetics*, ed. Ingram Bywater, Oxford: Clarendon Press.

Bakhtin, M. Mikhail (1981) *The Dialogic Imagination: Four Essays*, trans. Caryl Emerson and Michael Holquist, ed. Michael Holquist, Slavic Series, Austin: University of Texas Press.

—— (1973) *Problems of Dostoevsky's Poetics*, trans. R. W. Rotsel, Ann Arbor, MI: Ardis.

Balderston, Daniel, Mike Gonzalez and Ana López (eds) (2000) *Encyclopedia of Contemporary Latin American and Caribbean Cultures*, London: Routledge.

Belsey, Catherine (1980) *Critical Practice*, London and New York: Methuen.

Bleiberg, German, Maureen Ihrie and Janet Pérez (eds) (1993) *Dictionary of the Literature of the Iberian Peninsula*, Westport, CT: Greenwood Press.

Boehmer, Elleke (1995) *Colonial and Postcolonial Literature: Migrant Metaphors*, Oxford: Oxford University Press.

Brennan, Timothy (1989) *Salman Rushdie and the Third World: Myths of the Nation*, Houndmills, Basingstoke: Macmillan.

Bruchac, Joseph (ed.) (1987) 'Interview with Simon Ortiz', in *Survival This Way: Interviews with American Indian Poets*, Tucson: Sun Tracks and University of Arizona Press.

Carol, Lewis [1865] (1929) *Alice in Wonderland and Through the Looking Glass etc.*, Everyman's Library, London: J. M. Dent and Sons.

Carter, Angela (1989) 'Introduction: Frida Kahlo', in *Images of Frida Kahlo*, London: Redstone.

Cervantes, Miguel de Saavedra (1992) *Don Quixote de la Mancha*, trans. Charles Jarvis, ed. E. C. Riley, World Classics Series, Oxford: Oxford University Press.

Chaucer, Geoffrey [1387] (1974) 'The Canterbury Tales', in F. N. Robinson (ed.) *The Works of Geoffrey Chaucer*, Oxford: Oxford University Press.

Cixous, Hélène (1989) 'Sorties: Out and Out: Attacks/Ways Out/Forays', in Catherine Belsey and Jane Moore (eds) *The Feminist Reader: Essays in Gender and the Politics of Literary Criticism*, Houndmills, Basingstoke: Macmillan.

Cornwell, Neil (1990) *The Literary Fantastic: From Gothic to Postmodernism*, Hemel Hempstead: Harvester Wheatsheaf.

Crockett, Dennis (1999) *German Post-Expressionism: The Art of the Great Disorder, 1918–1924*, University Park, PA: Pennsylvania State University Press.

Dalí, Salvador (1931) *The Persistence of Memory*, Museum of Modern Art, New York.

Davies, Norman (1996) *Europe: A History*, Oxford: Oxford University Press.

De Beauvoir, Simone (1993) *The Second Sex*, trans. H. M. Parshley, Everyman's Library, London: D. Campbell.

Dombroski, Robert (1996) 'The Rise and Fall of Facism', in Peter Brand and Lino Pertile (eds) *The Cambridge History of Italian Literature*, Cambridge: Cambridge University Press.

Ebert, Roger (no date) 'Wings of Desire – Wim Wenders', Montreal: Goethe Institute. Available online. HTTP: http://www.goethe.de/uk/mon/archiv/ewenders/ewings.htm (accessed 10 February 2002).

Evans, Mari (ed.) (1985) *Black Women Writers: Arguments and Interviews*, London: Pluto.

Fanon, Frantz (1967) *The Wretched of the Earth*, trans. Constance Farrington, Harmondsworth, Middlesex: Pelican/Penguin.

Ferguson, Rebecca (1991) 'History, Memory and Language in Toni Morrison's *Beloved*', in Susan Sellers (ed.) *Feminist Criticism: Theory and Practice*, New York: Harvester Wheatsheaf, pp. 109–27.

Fowlie, Wallace (1960) *Age of Surrealism*. Bloomington and London: Indiana University Press.

Fuentes, Carlos (1995) 'Introduction', in Frida Kahlo, *The Diary of Frida Kahlo: An Intimate Self-Portrait*, London: Bloomsbury.

Fujita Sato, Gayle K. (1991) 'Ghosts as Chinese-American Constructs in Maxine Hong Kingston's The Woman Warrior', in Lynette Carpenter and Wendy Kolmar (eds) *Haunting the House of Fiction*, Knoxville: University of Tennessee Press, pp. 193–214.

Gates, Henry Louis, Jr.(1988) *The Signifying Monkey: A Theory of African American Criticism*, Oxford: Oxford University Press.

Gilroy, Paul (1993) *Small Acts: Thoughts on the Politics of Black Cultures*, London: Serpents Tail.

Grant, David (1970) *Realism*, New Critical Idiom Series, London: Methuen.

Gunning, Tom (1999) 'Narrative Discourse and the Narrator System', in Leo Braudy and Marshall Cohen (eds) *Film Theory and Criticism: Introductory Readings* (5th edn), New York and Oxford: Oxford University Press, pp. 461–72.

Hunt, Peter (1991) *Criticism, Theory and Children's Literature*, Oxford: Basil Blackwell.

Hutcheon, Linda (1988) *A Poetics of Postmodernism: History, Theory, Fiction*, London: Routledge.

Huxley, Aldous [1932] (1952) *Brave New World*, London: Vanguard Library.

James, Henry [1898] (1986) 'The Turn of the Screw', in *The Aspern Papers and The Turn of the Screw*, London: Penguin, pp. 145–262.

—— [1934] (1992) 'Henry James on the Art of Fiction', in Lillian Furst, *Realism*, London: Longman, pp. 43–4.

Jameson, Fredric (1991) *Postmodernism or, The Cultural Logic of Late Capitalism*, London: Verso.

Kafka, Franz [1915] (1961) 'Metamorphosis', in *Metamorphosis and Other Stories*, trans. Willa and Edwin Muir, Harmondsworth, Middlesex: Penguin.

King, John (1990) *Magical Reels: A History of Cinema in Latin America*, London and New York: Verson.

LeClair, Thomas (1994) 'The Language Must Not Sweat: A Conversation with Toni Morrison', in Danille Taylor-Guthrie (ed.) *Conversations with Toni Morrison*, Jackson: University Press of Mississippi.

Lindstrom, Naomi (1994) *Twentieth-Century Spanish American Fiction*, Austin: University of Texas Press.

Lyotard, Jean-François [1979] (1984) *The Postmodern Condition: A Report on Knowledge*, trans. Geoff Bennington and Brian Massumi, Theory and History of Literature 10, Manchester: Manchester University Press.

McCaughrean, Geraldine (1982) *One Thousand and One Arabian Nights*, Oxford: Oxford University Press.

McHale, Brian (1987) *Postmodernist Fiction*, New York and London: Methuen.

McLeod, John (2000) *Beginning Postcolonialism*, Manchester and New York: Manchester University Press.

Marx, Karl (1977) *Selected Writings of Karl Marx*, ed. David McLellan, Oxford: Oxford University Press.

Minta, Stephen (1987) *García Márquez: Writer of Columbia*, New York: Harper and Row.

Ousby, Ian (ed.) (1993) *The Cambridge Guide to Literature in English*, Cambridge: Cambridge University Press.

Pollard, Arthur (1970) *Satire*, Critical Idiom Series, London: Methuen.

Pope, Randolph D. (1996) 'The Spanish American Novel from 1950 to 1975', in Robert González Echevarría and Enrique Pupo-Walker, *The Cambridge History of Latin American Literature: The Twentieth Century, Vol. 2*, Cambridge: Cambridge University Press, pp. 226–78.

Price, Greg (1990) *Latin America: The Writer's Journey*, London: Hamish Hamilton.

Reder, Michael R. (2000) *Conversations with Salman Rushdie*, Literary Conversations Series, Jackson: University Press of Mississippi.

Roberts, Adam (2000) *Science Fiction*, New Critical Idiom Series, London: Routledge.

Said, Edward (1979) *Orientalism*, New York: Random House.

Sale, Maggie (1992) 'Call and Response as Critical Method: African American Oral Traditions and *Beloved*', *African American Review*, **26**, 1: 47–50.

Stallybrass, Peter and Allon White (1986) *The Politics and Poetics of Transgression*, London: Methuen.

Sterne, Laurence [1769] (1983) *The Life and Opinions of Tristram Shandy, Gentleman*, Oxford: Clarendon Press.

Swanson, Philip (1995) *The New Novel in Latin America: Politics and Popular Culture After the Boom*, Manchester and New York: Manchester University Press.

Swift, Jonathon [1726] (1967) *Gulliver's Travels*, Peter Dixon and John Chalker (eds), Harmondsworth, Middlesex: Penguin.

Todorov, Tzvetan (1975) *The Fantastic: A Structural Approach to a Literary Genre*, trans. Richard Howard, Ithaca, NY: Cornell University Press.

Tonkin, Elizabeth (1990) 'History and the Myth of Realism', in Raphael Samuel and Paul Thompson (eds) *The Myths We Live By*, London: Routledge, pp. 25–35.

Vautier, Marie (1998) *New World Myth: Postmodernism and Postcolonialism in Canadian Fiction*, Montreal and Kingston: McGill-Queen's University Press.

Verani, Hugo J. (1996) 'The *Vanguardia* and its Implications', in Robert González Echevarría and Enrique Pupo-Walker, *The Cambridge History of Latin American Literature: The Twentieth Century, Vol. 2*, Cambridge: Cambridge University Press, pp. 114–37.

Watt, Ian [1957] (1992) 'Ian Watt on Realism and the Novel Form', in Lilian Furst, *Realism*, London: Longman, pp. 87–94.

Williams, Raymond L. (1985) *Gabriel García Márquez*, Boston, MA: Twayne Publishers.

INDEX

Note: References in **bold** are to the Glossary